CW00348351

Collins

11+
Maths

Practice Papers
Book 1

Simon Greaves

Introduction

The 11+ tests

In most cases, the 11+ selection tests are set by GL Assessment (NFER), CEM or the individual school. You should be able to find out which tests your child will be taking on the website of the school they are applying to or from the local authority.

These single subject practice test papers are designed to reflect the style of GL Assessment tests, but provide useful practice and preparation for all 11+ tests and common entrance exams.

The score achieved on these test papers is no guarantee that your child will achieve a score of the same standard on the formal tests. Other factors, such as the standard of responses from all pupils who took the test, will determine their success in the formal examination.

Collins also publishes practice test papers, in partnership with The 11 Plus Tutoring Academy, to support preparation for the CEM tests.

Contents

This book contains:

- four practice papers – Tests A, B, C and D

- a multiple-choice answer sheet for each test

- a complete set of answers, including explanations.

Further multiple-choice answer sheets can be downloaded from our website so that you can reuse these papers: collins.co.uk/11plus

Maths

Mathematics tests are used by schools to assess the ability of each child and determine whether they have attained the required standard of mathematical skills, reasoning and problem-solving.

It is particularly important to provide maths practice as the 11+ tests may test skills that are slightly more advanced than those on the national curriculum for your child's age.

The importance of practice

Practice will help your child to do his or her best on the day of the tests. Working through a number of practice tests allows your child to practise answering a range of test-style questions. It also provides an opportunity to learn how to manage time effectively, so that time is not wasted during the test and any 'extra' time is used constructively for checking.

Getting ready for the tests

If your child is unfamiliar with mathematics 11+ papers, it may be advisable to attempt a few questions first without time constraints and give your child the opportunity to ask questions and receive some initial feedback.

It is best to do the tests at a time when your child is alert and able to concentrate fully on them. Tiredness and other distractions will have an adverse effect on their performance. Spend some time talking with your child before the test so that they understand the purpose of the practice papers.

It is also good to go through with your child some tactics to adopt when attempting the paper. These might include:

- Work quickly and carefully through the questions.

- All the questions are worth equal marks, so don't spend too long on any one question.

- If you get stuck, leave it and then come back to it if you have time.

- If you have spare time at the end, go back and check your answers. Every mark counts!

Administering the tests

Make sure that the surroundings are appropriate and quiet. Your child will need a pencil and rubber and some paper for rough working. A calculator must not be used.

Allow your child some time at the start to read the information on the front of the paper.

Each mathematics test consists of 50 questions to be completed in 50 minutes. It is essential that your child is able to work uninterrupted for this time. A clock should be provided so that a check can be kept on the time left.

Multiple-choice tests

For this style of test, the answers are recorded on a separate answer sheet and not in the book. This answer sheet will often be marked by a computer in the actual exam, so it is important that it is used correctly. Answers should be indicated by drawing a clear pencil line through the appropriate box and there should be no other marks. If your child indicates one answer and then wants to change their response, the first mark must be fully rubbed out. Practising with an answer sheet now will reduce the chance of your child getting anxious or confused during the actual test.

Marking

Award one mark for each correct answer. Do not award any marks for correct working with an incorrect answer, or any half-marks.

It is important that you start by providing some positive feedback for questions that have been correctly answered. This will help your child to identify the topics that they are confident with. Next, identify questions where your child has made an easily correctable mistake or misread the question. Ask your child to try these questions again to see if correct answers can be obtained. Finally, identify the questions that your child provided incorrect answers for, or was unable to answer at all. Revise the material covered by these questions and re-attempt them.

And finally...

Let your child know that tests are just one part of school life and that doing their best is what matters. Plan a fun incentive for after the 11+ tests, such as a day out.

Contents

ACKNOWLEDGEMENTS

The author and publisher are grateful to the copyright holders for permission to use quoted materials and images.

Every effort has been made to trace copyright holders and obtain their permission for the use of copyright material. The author and publisher will gladly receive information enabling them to rectify any error or omission in subsequent editions. All facts are correct at time of going to press.

Published by Collins
An imprint of HarperCollins*Publishers*
1 London Bridge Street
London SE1 9GF

HarperCollins*Publishers*
1st Floor, Watermarque Building
Ringsend Road
Dublin 4, Ireland

ISBN 9781844197163

First published 2010
This edition 2020
Previously published as Letts

9

Text, design and Illustration
© HarperCollins*Publishers* Ltd 2020

All rights reserved. No part of this publication may be reproduced, stored in a retrieval system, or transmitted, in any form or by any means, electronic, mechanical, photocopying, recording or otherwise, without the prior permission of Collins.

British Library Cataloguing in Publication Data.

A CIP record of this book is available from the British Library.

Commissioning Editor: Rebecca Skinner
Author: Simon Greaves
Project Manager: Michael Appleton
Editorial: Catherine Dakin
Cover Design: Kevin Robbins and Sarah Duxbury
Printed and bound in the UK using 100% Renewable Electricity at CPI Group (UK) Ltd

MIX
Paper from
responsible source
FSC
www.fsc.org   FSC™ C007454

This book is produced from independently certified FSC™ paper to ensure responsible forest management.

For more information visit:
www.harpercollins.co.uk/green

Mathematics
Multiple-Choice
Practice Test A

Read the following carefully:

1. You must not open or turn over this booklet until you are told to do so.

2. This is a multiple-choice test, which contains a number of different types of questions.

3. You may do any rough working on a separate sheet of paper.

4. Answers should be marked on the answer sheet provided, not on the test booklet.

5. If you make a mistake, rub it out as completely as you can and put in your new answer.

6. Work as carefully and as quickly as you can. If you cannot do a question, do not waste time on it but go on to the next.

7. If you are not sure of an answer, choose the one you think is best.

8. You will have 50 minutes to complete the test.

1. There are thirty thousand, four hundred and seventy-four people at a football match.

   What is this number written in figures?

   34,474   30,704   30,474   3,474   30,744

2. Jake has one £2 coin, five 50p coins, three 10p coins and five 5p coins.

   How much money does he have?

3. Which of the shapes is **not** a quadrilateral?

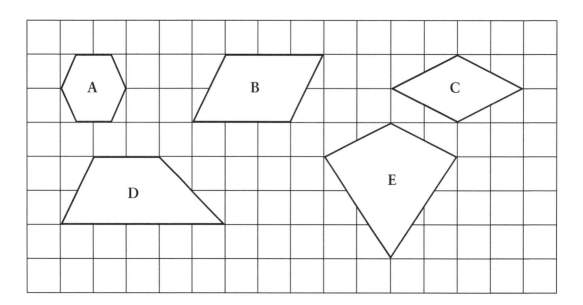

4. Peaches cost 58p each.

   How much will 9 peaches cost?

5. Here is a list of scores in a spelling test.

   12   14   11   8   14   8   14   12   16

   What is the modal score?

6. Which number lies half-way between 46 and 84?

7. The time on an analogue clock shows 2.45 p.m.

   How would this be written as a 24-hour clock time?

   12:45   02:45   14:45   16:45   08:45

8. Which of these numbers is **not** a square number?

   25   81   64   48   16

9. Carrots cost 35p per kilogram and potatoes cost 40p per kilogram.

    Mr Price buys 2 kg of carrots and 1 kg of potatoes.

    How much does Mr Price spend?

10. Which number is exactly divisible by 5 and 9?

    27   40   55   90   105

11. How many dots are needed to make the next pattern in the sequence?

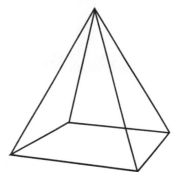

12. Which number has the highest value?

    1.14   0.33   1.03   1.3   0.43

13. Name the 3D shape.

    A   tetrahedron

    B   cone

    C   triangular prism

    D   square-based pyramid

    E   equilateral triangle

14. A gardener sows 360 seeds in trays.

    He puts the same number of seeds in each tray.

    If he uses 6 trays, how many seeds are in each tray?

15. Which of these numbers does **not** give 3.88 when rounded to two decimal places?

    3.8808   3.88402   3.8796   3.8715   3.875055

16. The table shows the number of burgers sold in a takeaway.

	Size		
	Small	Medium	Large
Hamburger	35	54	18
Cheeseburger	?	42	?

The takeaway sold half as many small cheeseburgers as they sold medium hamburgers.

Also, thirteen more large cheeseburgers than small cheeseburgers were sold.

How many burgers did the takeaway sell in total?

17. A box of chocolates weighs 415 grams and contains 24 chocolates.

The empty box weighs 55 grams.

What is the weight of one chocolate?

18. Which of the shapes has exactly 2 lines of symmetry and rotational symmetry of order 2?

| A | B | C | D | E |

19. What is $1\frac{7}{10}$ as a decimal?

| 0.17 | 1.7 | 0.7 | 7.1 | 1.07 |

20. What are the co-ordinates of the point marked P?

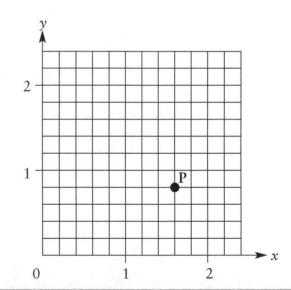

21. Chloe's cat weighs 2700 grams.

What is the cat's weight in kilograms?

22. Kieran leaves the house to go swimming at 14:55.

He returns home 1 hour and 30 minutes later.

What time does he return?

17:25   16:30   16:25   15:45   16:15

23. There are 52 seeds in a packet.

How many seeds are there in 18 packets?

24. A person is standing at X and follows the instructions below.

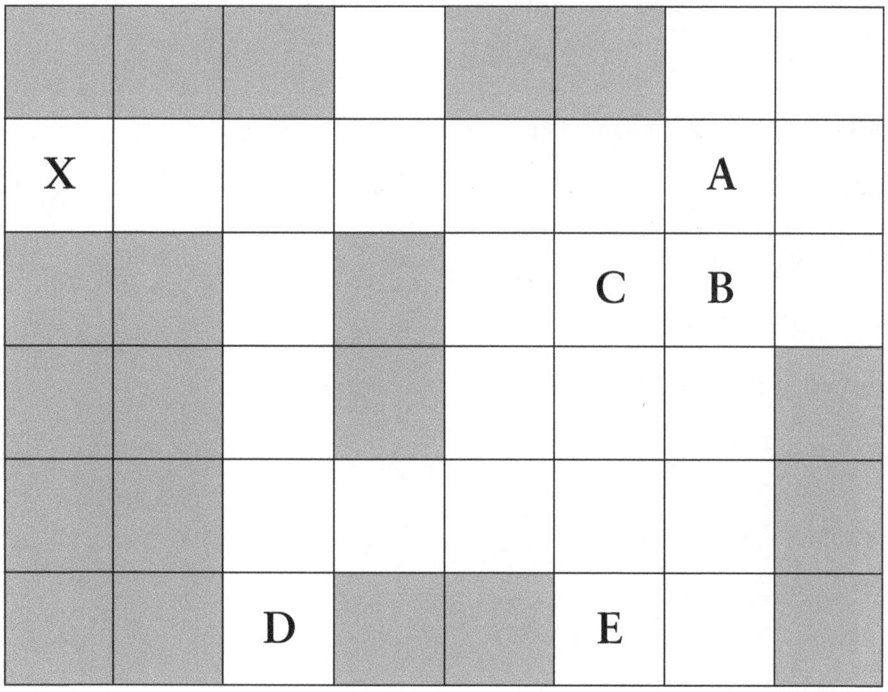

FORWARD 4, TURN RIGHT 90°

FORWARD 3, TURN LEFT 90°

FORWARD 2, TURN LEFT 90°

FORWARD 2

Which letter do the instructions take the person to?

25. The bar chart shows the weights of a group of people.

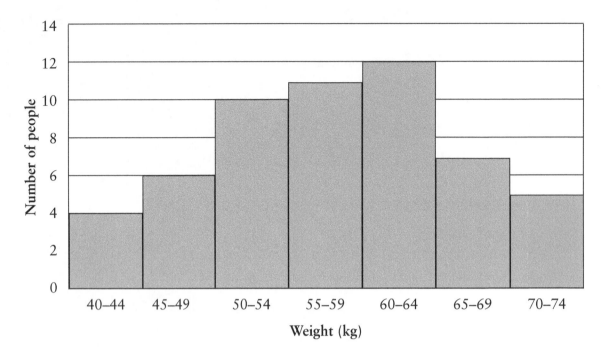

Which one of the following statements is true?

A 2 people weigh 40–44 kg.

B 24 people weigh 60 kg or more.

C 16 people weigh less than 55 kg.

D 12 people weigh between 50 and 54 kg.

E 10 people weigh more than 50 kg.

26. In a class of 30 children, 12 are boys.

What percentage of the class are girls?

27. Outside an aircraft, the temperature is –24°C.

Inside the aircraft, the temperature is 18°C.

What is the difference between the temperatures?

28. What is the approximate size of angle x in the diagram?

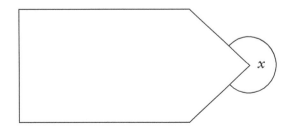

29. Four brothers have a mean age of 10.

Three of the brothers are aged 7, 11 and 14.

What is the age of the fourth brother?

30. There are 12 girls in a class of 28 children.

What is the ratio of girls to boys?

31. Peter thinks of a number.

He adds 3 to the number, then multiplies his answer by 4.

He then subtracts 12.

His final answer is 60.

What was the number Peter first thought of?

32. Sarah has 35 paperback books and 20 hardback books.

What fraction of the books are hardbacks?

33. Calculate the area of the shape.

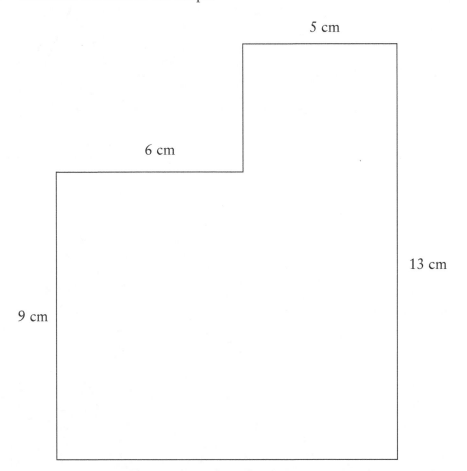

34. Here are two spinners.

Spinner A

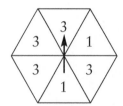

Spinner B

Which one of the following statements is true?

A It is more likely to spin a 3 on spinner A than on spinner B.

B It is equally likely to spin a 3 on spinner A and spinner B.

C It is more likely to spin a 3 on spinner B than on spinner A.

D It is less likely to spin a 1 on spinner B than spinner A.

E It is less likely to spin a 2 on spinner A than on spinner B.

35. Which pair of triangles are congruent?

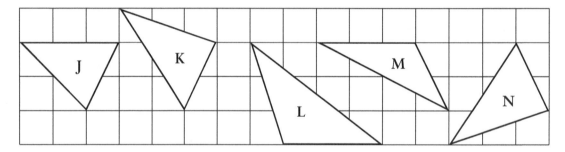

A J and K

B L and M

C K and N

D L and N

E K and L

36. Which of these fractions has the highest value?

$\dfrac{3}{5}$ $\qquad\qquad$ $\dfrac{3}{10}$ $\qquad\qquad$ $\dfrac{3}{4}$ $\qquad\qquad$ $\dfrac{7}{8}$ $\qquad\qquad$ $\dfrac{7}{9}$

37. What number is the arrow pointing to?

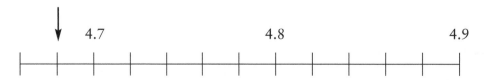

38. Boris is t years old.

Kyle is 5 years older than Boris.

Ian is three times as old as Kyle.

Which expression gives Ian's age?

$3t$ $t + 5$ $3t + 5$ $3t + 15$ $5t + 3$

39. Which has the greatest value?

30% of 320 $\frac{1}{3}$ of 330   33% of 300   0.3 of 320 $\frac{3}{10}$ of 310

40. The distance from Durham to Leeds is about 80 miles.

About how many kilometres is this?

41. A taxi company has 18 taxis.

On average, each taxi takes 19 fares a day.

The typical cost of a taxi fare is £5.

Estimate the total money taken in fares by the taxi company in one day.

42. What is the value of $16^2 - 12^2$?

43. Laura runs 6 times around a trail that measures 2.35 kilometres.

Ravi runs 4 times around a trail that measures 3550 metres. Who runs furthest and by how much?

A   Laura by 200 metres

B   Laura by 250 metres

C   Ravi by 100 metres

D   Ravi by 200 metres

E   Laura by 100 metres

44. A TV has had its price reduced by 20% in a sale.

The sale price of the TV is £160.

What was the original price of the TV?

NOW GO ON TO THE NEXT PAGE

45. The perimeter of a rectangle is 24 cm. The length of each side is a whole number of centimetres.

Which of these areas can the rectangle **not** have?

35 cm²   27 cm²   32 cm²   28 cm²   20 cm²

46. What is the size of the angle marked x?

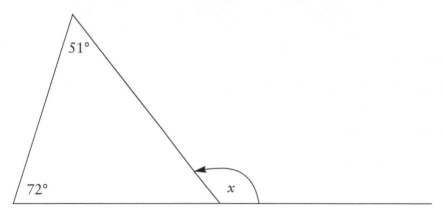

47. $(32 \times 24) - 80 = 688$

Which of the following is incorrect?

$(32 \times 24) - 60 = 708$

$80 + 688 = 32 \times 24$

$(31 \times 24) - 56 = 688$

$80 = (32 \times 24) - 688$

$(31 \times 24) + 24 = 688$

48. What is the perimeter of the shape?

$2c + a + b$

$2a + 2b + 2c$

$a + b + c$

abc

$ac + bc$

49. Here is an equation:

$4n + 15 = 45 - 2n$

What is the value of n?

50. The pie chart shows the proportion of hot drinks sold in a café one day.

150 cups of coffee were sold.

How many cups of chocolate were sold?

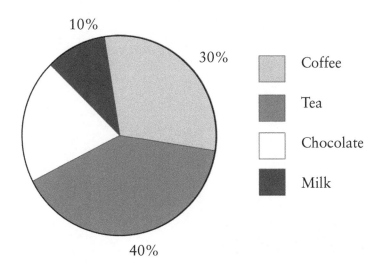

TEST ADVICE

This information will not appear in the actual test.
It is included here to remind you not to stop working
until you are told the test is over.

CHECK YOUR ANSWERS AGAIN IF THERE IS TIME

FINDING ONE MISTAKE CAN MEAN EXTRA MARKS

Mathematics
Multiple-Choice
Practice Test B

Read the following carefully:

1. You must not open or turn over this booklet until you are told to do so.

2. This is a multiple-choice test, which contains a number of different types of questions.

3. You may do any rough working on a separate sheet of paper.

4. Answers should be marked on the answer sheet provided, not on the test booklet.

5. If you make a mistake, rub it out as completely as you can and put in your new answer.

6. Work as carefully and as quickly as you can. If you cannot do a question, do not waste time on it but go on to the next.

7. If you are not sure of an answer, choose the one you think is best.

8. You will have 50 minutes to complete the test.

1. What is the number 8 worth in this number?

    18,674

2. Which of these shapes is a right-angled triangle?

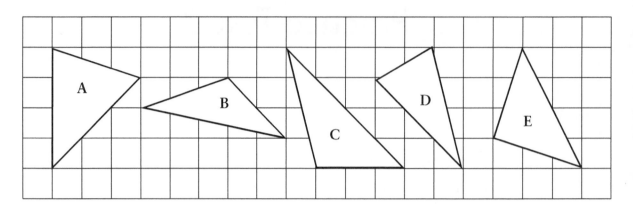

3. Mrs Carter buys a music CD and a DVD film.

    The total cost is £19.76.

    The CD costs £7.98. How much does the DVD cost?

4. One day in January, the temperature in London was –1°C at midday.

    The temperature in Moscow was 11 degrees colder.

    What was the temperature in Moscow?

5. A TV programme starts at 15:35 and finishes at 16:50.

    How long does the programme last?

6. The pictogram shows the different types of tree in a wood.

Key: ⊞ represents 20 trees	
Oak	⊟
Pine	⊞ ⊞ ⊞
Sycamore	⊞ ⊞ ▫
Birch	⊞ ⊞ ⊟
Elm	⊞ ⊞

How many more birch trees are there than oak trees in the wood?

7. What is the name of this 2D shape?

8. Twenty-six thousand and forty-eight spectators watched a rugby match. What is this number written in figures?

9. Which number is incorrectly placed in the sorting diagram?

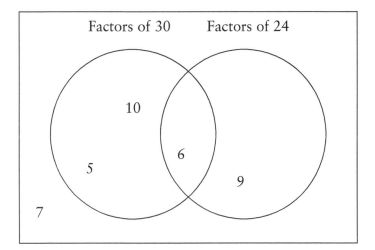

10. What is the answer when 525 is divided by 5?

11. Which triangle has three acute angles?

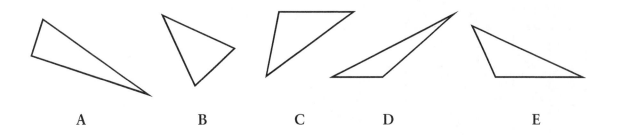

A   B   C   D   E

12. Here is a sequence:

    12   17   15   20   18   ?

    What is the next number in the sequence?

13. The bar chart shows the marks scored by a group of 20 children in a spelling test.

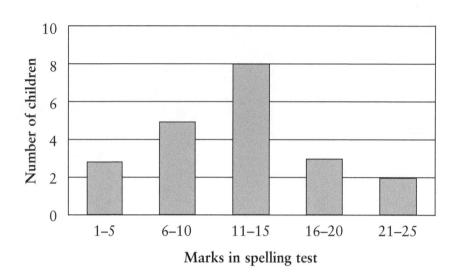

How many children scored fewer than 11 marks?

14. Which of these numbers is **not** a multiple of 15?

30   90   70   75   45

15. A robot is placed on a grid at X.

The robot is programmed with the following instructions:

FORWARD 5, TURN RIGHT 90°

FORWARD 3, TURN RIGHT 90°

FORWARD 3, TURN LEFT 90°

FORWARD 1

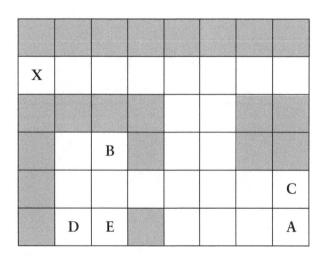

To which letter will the instructions take the robot?

16. Which of these shapes does **not** have any lines of symmetry?

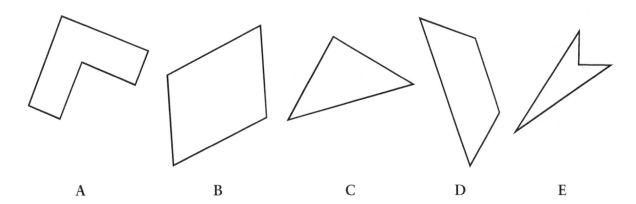

A   B   C   D   E

17. Jagjeet buys one small ham pizza and one large pepperoni pizza.

Pizza	Small	Large
Cheese pizza	£2.75	£3.25
Ham pizza	£3.80	£4.45
Pepperoni pizza	£4.35	£4.90
Salad	60p	90p

How much change will he get from a £10 note?

18. The table shows the number of tickets sold for a show in a small theatre for four different nights.

	Wednesday	Thursday	Friday	Saturday
Stalls	45	52	70	110
Circle	40	63	65	76
Gallery	25	21	24	41

How many more tickets were sold for the show on Saturday than were sold for Thursday?

19. Which number lies half-way between 24 and 38?

20. Which of these weights is the most likely weight of a 50p coin?

200 grams   8 grams   1 gram   40 grams   800 grams

21. A school trip costs £26 per child.

18 pupils are going on the trip.

The pupils have raised £324 towards the cost of the trip.

How much more money do they need to cover the cost of the trip?

22. The line AB and the point C are shown on the grid.

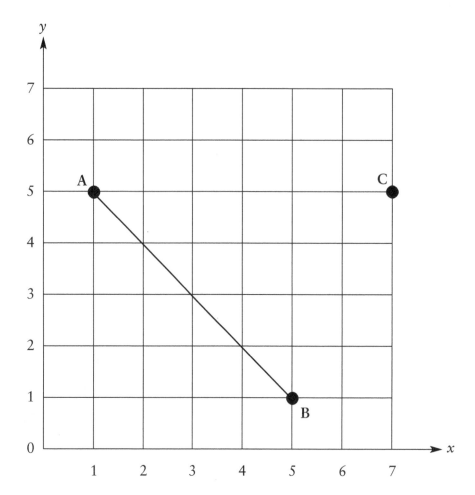

Which point must be plotted and joined to C to make a line that is perpendicular to the line AB?

(3, 1)   (5, 7)   (6, 1)   (1, 3)   (4, 3)

23. A farmer has a rectangular field which has a width of 28 metres and a length of 34 metres.

He is planning to put a fence around the perimeter of the field.

What length of fencing does he need?

24. Which of these nets folds to make this cube?

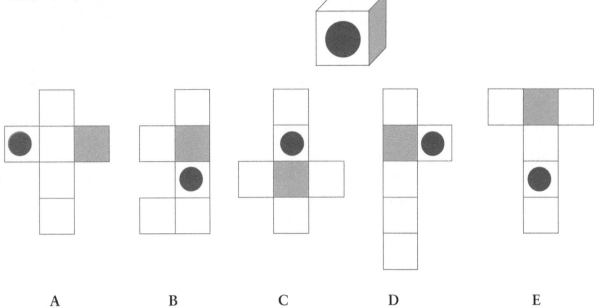

| A | B | C | D | E |

25. This machine multiplies a number by 4 and then adds 1.

Which number has been put into the machine?

26. Here is a diagram that can be used to sort chocolates.

Which statement should be written in the blank space?

A Is it a milk chocolate?

B Is it a chocolate?

C Is it a toffee?

D Is it a plain chocolate?

E Is it a mint?

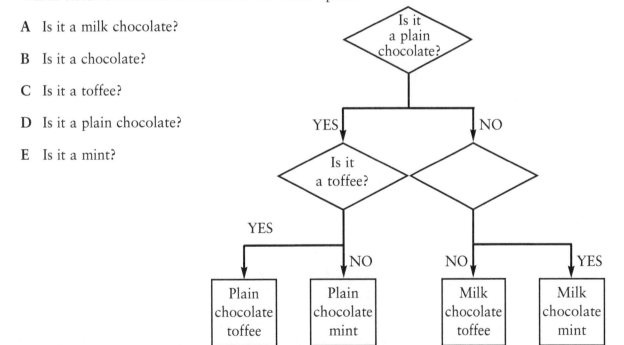

27. Look at this number line.

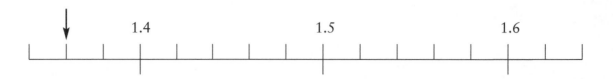

What number does the arrow point to?

28. Paul is four times as old as his brother.

In six years' time Paul will be eighteen.

How old will his brother be in six years' time?

29. A coach can carry 32 passengers.

How many coaches are needed to carry 448 passengers?

30. A group of nine children record their shoe size.

Here are the results:

2   3   3   5   6   4   3   4   6

What is the mean shoe size of the nine children?

31. What is the approximate size of the angle marked a?

70°   90°   100°   140°   45°

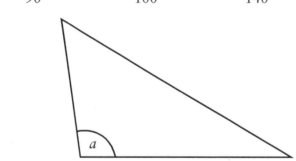

32. What percentage of the diagram is shaded?

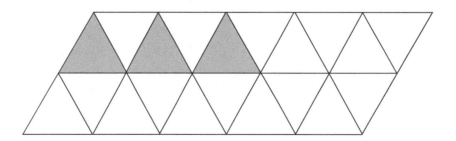

33. A bag contains 11 balls.

There are 5 red balls, 2 blue balls and the rest of the balls are white.

A ball is taken from the bag at random.

What is the probability that the ball is either red or white?

34. What is 15% of 580 kg?

35. What is this number correct to two decimal places?

9.21563

36. A grapefruit is weighed on some kitchen scales.

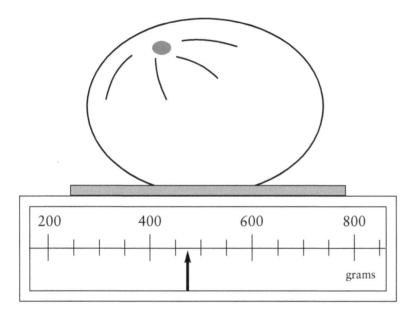

What is the weight of the grapefruit?

37. Here are the ingredients for a recipe to make 10 shortbread biscuits.

150 grams of flour
100 grams of butter
50 grams of sugar

Oliver wants to make 25 shortbread biscuits.

How much flour will he need?

38. The points P and Q are shown in the grid.

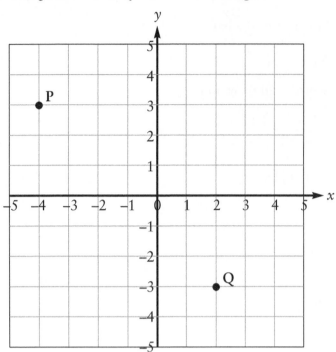

What are the co-ordinates of P and Q?

A   P (–3, 4)   Q (–3, 2)

B   P (4, 3)   Q (2, 3)

C   P (–4, 0)   Q (2, 0)

D   P (–4, 3)   Q (2, –3)

E   P (–4, –3)   Q (–2, –3)

39. Mark the letter that shows these fractions in order of size, starting with the smallest.

$\frac{5}{6}$ $\frac{2}{3}$ $\frac{3}{4}$ $\frac{5}{8}$

A $\frac{2}{3}$, $\frac{3}{4}$, $\frac{5}{6}$, $\frac{5}{8}$

B $\frac{3}{4}$, $\frac{5}{8}$, $\frac{5}{6}$, $\frac{2}{3}$

C $\frac{2}{3}$, $\frac{3}{4}$, $\frac{5}{8}$, $\frac{5}{6}$

D $\frac{5}{8}$, $\frac{2}{3}$, $\frac{3}{4}$, $\frac{5}{6}$

E $\frac{5}{8}$, $\frac{3}{4}$, $\frac{2}{3}$, $\frac{5}{6}$

40.

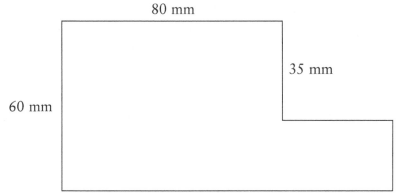

What is the area of this shape in cm²?

41. The scale on a map is 1:125 000.

What actual distance in kilometres is represented by 2 cm on the map?

42. Here are the hours that Mr Peel has worked so far this week.

Day	Number of hours
Monday	7
Tuesday	8
Wednesday	5
Thursday	7
Friday	6
Saturday	?

How many hours must Mr Peel work on Saturday so that the mean number of hours he has worked this week is 6 hours?

43. Which number is closest in value to 3?

2.995　　　　　3.01　　　　　2.98　　　　　3.099　　　　　3.1

44. Gemma is n years old and 5 years older than Claire. Claire is 7 years older than Zoe.

Which expression gives Zoe's age?

12　　　　　$n + 5$　　　　　$n - 7$　　　　　$n + 12$　　　　　$n - 12$

45. What number should replace the * in the number grid?

3	9	27
9	27	81
27	81	*

46. Which of these gives the fraction $\frac{24}{80}$ in its lowest terms?

$\frac{1}{3}$ $\qquad\qquad$ $\frac{3}{10}$ $\qquad\qquad$ $\frac{2}{5}$ $\qquad\qquad$ $\frac{12}{40}$ $\qquad\qquad$ $\frac{1}{4}$

47. This is a regular pentagon.

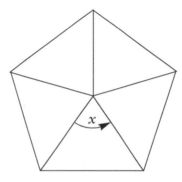

What is the size of the angle marked x in the diagram?

48. In a street, the refuse bins are emptied every 9 days.

The recycling boxes are emptied every 5 days.

Both the bins and boxes are emptied together on the 1st March.

How many times will both the bins and the boxes be emptied on the same day from the 1st March to the 31st May?

49. $a + 2b = 5c$

Which of the following statements is incorrect?

$2a + 4b = 10c$ $\qquad$ $5c - a = 2b$ $\qquad$ $a = 5c + 2b$ $\qquad$ $2b - 5c + a = 0$ $\qquad$ $4b = 10c - 2a$

50. What is the area of the shape?

$2yz + xy$

$x(y + 2z)$

$xy + xz$

xyz

$x + 2y + 2z$

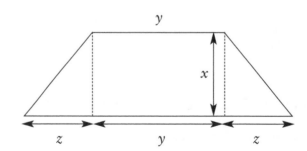

Mathematics
Multiple-Choice
Practice Test C

Read the following carefully:

1. You must not open or turn over this booklet until you are told to do so.

2. This is a multiple-choice test, which contains a number of different types of questions.

3. You may do any rough working on a separate sheet of paper.

4. Answers should be marked on the answer sheet provided, not on the test booklet.

5. If you make a mistake, rub it out as completely as you can and put in your new answer.

6. Work as carefully and as quickly as you can. If you cannot do a question, do not waste time on it but go on to the next.

7. If you are not sure of an answer, choose the one you think is best.

8. You will have 50 minutes to complete the test.

1. The population of a small town is 13,045.

   What is this number written in words?

   A   thirty thousand and forty-five

   B   thirteen thousand, four hundred and five

   C   one thousand, three hundred and forty-five

   D   one hundred thousand, three hundred and forty-five

   E   thirteen thousand and forty-five

2. The bar chart shows the number of sunny days in five months.

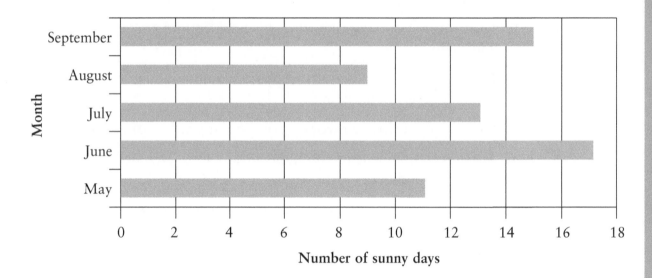

   How many more sunny days were there in June than in August?

3. Which of these shapes is **not** a pentagon?

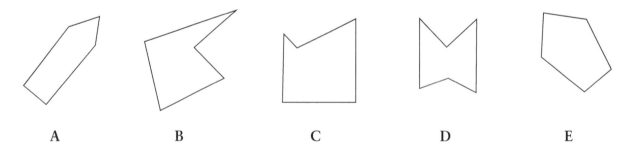

   A   B   C   D   E

4. What is the answer when 560 is divided by 4?

5. Which of the following is the most likely capacity for a glass of milk?

    2 litres   250 millilitres   5 litres   800 millilitres   20 millilitres

6. 178 people get on a train in Newcastle.

    At York, 59 more people get on the train, whilst 67 people get off.

    How many people are now on the train?

7. The pictogram shows the number of CDs sold by a supermarket over five days.

Number of CDs	
Key: ⬤ represents 100 CDs	
Wednesday	⬤ ⬤ ⬤
Thursday	⬤ ⬤ ◖
Friday	⬤ ⬤ ⬤ ⬤ ⬤
Saturday	⬤ ⬤ ⬤ ⬤ ⬤ ◖
Sunday	⬤ ⬤ ⬤ ◖

    How many CDs were sold at the weekend?

8. Here is a sequence:

    19   12   5   –2   ?   ?

    What are the next two numbers in the sequence?

9. Kwame buys two T-shirts costing £3.50 each and one pair of socks costing £1.20.

    How much does he spend altogether?

10. The diagram shows part of a shape and two mirror lines.

    If the part of the shape is reflected in the
    two mirror lines, what letter is made?

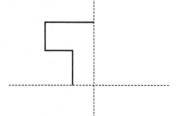

11. What are the co-ordinates of the point P?

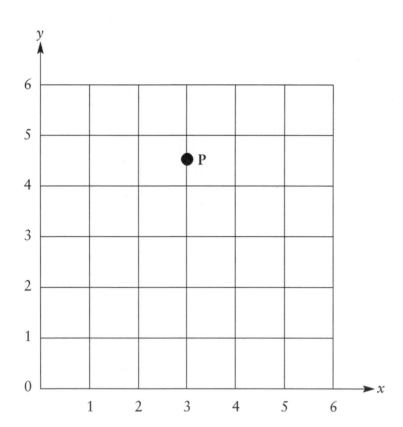

12. Mrs Ling made five cakes for a cake sale.

Here are the weights of the five cakes:

1.2 kg   1.05 kg   1.1 kg   1.25 kg   1.4 kg

What is the range?

13. Which of these decimal numbers is the largest?

2.89   2.9   2.98   2.08   2.0

14. This machine multiplies a number by 6 and then subtracts 17.

What number comes out of the machine?

11 ⟶  ⟶ ?

15. There are 60 minutes in one hour.

How many minutes are there in five and a half hours?

16. Which shape has a different area from the other four shapes?

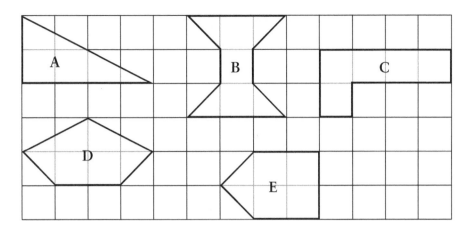

17. Which of these fractions is **not** equivalent to $\frac{4}{5}$?

$\frac{8}{10}$ $\qquad$ $\frac{15}{20}$ $\qquad$ $\frac{16}{20}$ $\qquad$ $\frac{40}{50}$ $\qquad$ $\frac{20}{25}$

18. Helen thinks of a number.

She adds 12 to the number then halves it.

She ends up with an answer of 34. What number did Helen think of?

19. Here is a patterned tile.

Which picture shows the tile when it has been rotated through 180°?

    A   B   C   D   E

20. A bag contains 200 coins.

10% of the coins are silver and the rest are copper.

How many silver coins are in the bag?

21. Lucy uses her mobile phone to send text messages.

Each text message costs 5p. She sends 60 messages in a week.

How much does she spend on text messages in a week?

22. A plan drawing of a house uses a scale of 1 centimetre to 4 metres.

The width of a room on the plan drawing measures 3.5 centimetres.

What is the actual width of the room?

23. What is the name of the 3D shape?

    A triangular prism

    B triangular-based pyramid

    C tetrahedron

    D triangle

    E trapezium

24. Roses cost £1.15 each and lilies cost 80p each.

How much does it cost to buy a bunch of five roses and four lilies?

25. What number should be written in place of the ? in the diagram?

80	88	96
96	104	?
104	?	120

26. This is the volume control on a radio.

Through which angle must the control be turned to change the volume from 5 to 2? Mark the correct answer on your sheet.

    A 135°

    B 45°

    C 90°

    D 180°

    E 120°

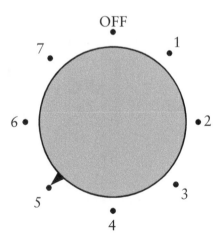

NOW GO ON TO THE NEXT PAGE

27. How many dots are in the two missing patterns?

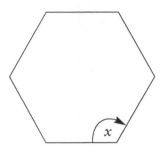

28. This is a regular hexagon. What is the size of angle x in the shape?

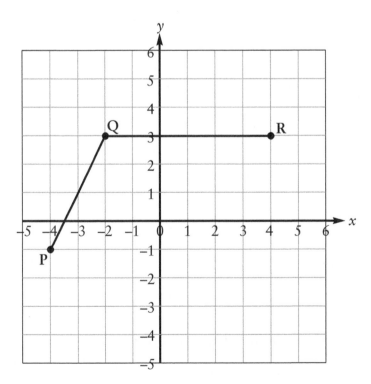

29. A milkshake is made using 4 spoonfuls of syrup and 300 millilitres of milk.

How many spoonfuls of syrup are needed for 750 millilitres of milk?

30. The points P, Q and R are plotted on a grid.

When a fourth point, S, is added and joined to P, Q and R they make a parallelogram.

What are the co-ordinates of S?

31. A jumper costing £12.50 is reduced by 30% in a sale.

What is the sale price of the jumper?

32. The graph converts pounds to dollars.

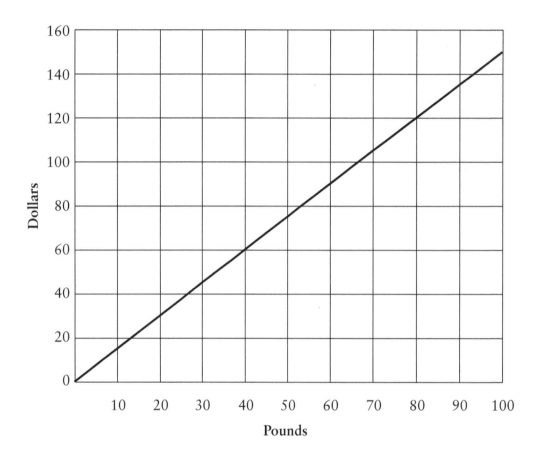

How many dollars would you get for 300 pounds?

33. A pizza takeaway delivered 161 pizzas in one week.

$\frac{3}{7}$ of the pizzas it delivered were pepperoni.

How many pepperoni pizzas were delivered in the week?

34. If $5x = y$, which of the following is **not** true?

$x = \frac{y}{5}$ $\qquad\qquad$ $\frac{y}{x} = 5$ $\qquad\qquad$ $10x = 2y$ $\qquad$ $y - x = 5$ $\qquad$ $0.2y = x$

35. There are 24 chocolates in a box.

12 are plain chocolate, 8 are milk chocolate and the rest are white chocolate.

What is the probability of picking a white chocolate?

36. Julia is saving to buy a bicycle costing £120.

She earns £15.50 for working in a shop each Saturday.

She has £24 in savings.

How many Saturdays must she work before she can afford to buy the bicycle?

37. Here are the prices of seven cars.

£7500   £5000   £6500   £7500   £7000   £8000   £5500

What is the median price?

38. There are 36 packets of paperclips in a box.

There are 300 paperclips in each packet.

How many paperclips are there in the box altogether?

39. What fraction of 2 litres is 600 millilitres?

40. Paul swims x lengths of a swimming pool on each weekday.

On Saturday and on Sunday he swims four more lengths than on a weekday.

How many lengths does Paul swim in one week?

$7x$ $5x + 4$ $7x + 8$ $7x + 4$ $5x$

41. The diagram shows the plan of a school hall.

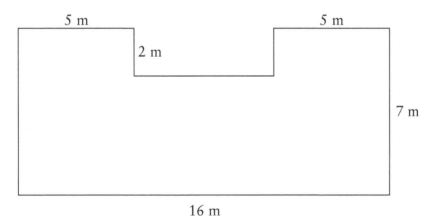

What is the area of the hall floor?

42. The ratio of boys to girls in a class of children is 3:5.

If there are 24 children in the class, how many girls are there?

43. The two angles x and $4x$ form a straight line. What is the value of x?

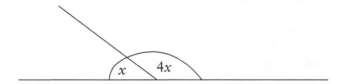

44. $8y - 24 = 40$

What is the value of y?

45. The pie chart shows the number of medals won by a country in the Olympic Games.

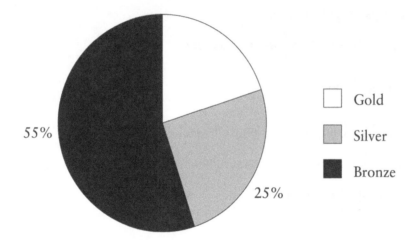

55%

25%

Gold

Silver

Bronze

80 athletes won a silver medal. How many athletes won a gold medal?

46. Which expression gives the area of the shape?

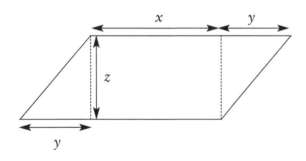

$x + y + z$ $z (x + y)$ $x (y + z)$ $xz + 2yz$ xyz

47. What is the answer when 5.2 is divided by 0.4?

48. The scale on a map is 1:125000.

What actual distance in kilometres is represented by 5 cm on the map?

49. Kira has some rectangular tiles and some equilateral triangle-shaped tiles.

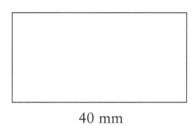

20 mm

20 mm

40 mm

She makes a shape with two rectangular tiles and two triangular tiles.

What is the perimeter of the shape she makes?

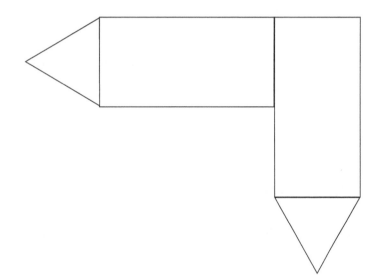

50. $2a = b$

Which of the following is **not** true?

$a + a = b$

$4a = 2b$

$2 = b + a$

$a = 0.5b$

$b = 2a$

TEST ADVICE

This information will not appear in the actual test.
It is included here to remind you not to stop working
until you are told the test is over.

CHECK YOUR ANSWERS AGAIN IF THERE IS TIME

FINDING ONE MISTAKE CAN MEAN EXTRA MARKS

Mathematics
Multiple-Choice
Practice Test D

Read the following carefully:

1. You must not open or turn over this booklet until you are told to do so.

2. This is a multiple-choice test, which contains a number of different types of questions.

3. You may do any rough working on a separate sheet of paper.

4. Answers should be marked on the answer sheet provided, not on the test booklet.

5. If you make a mistake, rub it out as completely as you can and put in your new answer.

6. Work as carefully and as quickly as you can. If you cannot do a question, do not waste time on it but go on to the next.

7. If you are not sure of an answer, choose the one you think is best.

8. You will have 50 minutes to complete the test.

1. What is the number when 4586 is rounded to the nearest ten?

2. The bar chart shows the eye colour of the children in a school.

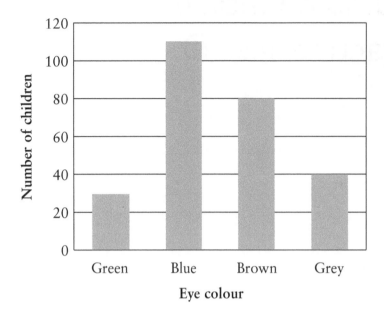

How many children do **not** have green eyes?

3. Which of these shapes is **not** a quadrilateral?

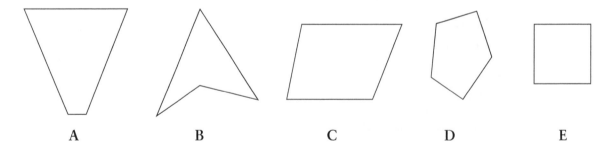

4. The table shows the number of medals won by a team at an athletics competition over three years.

	Gold	Silver	Bronze
2007	3	7	10
2008	6	5	11
2009	4	4	9

How many more medals did the team win in 2008 than in 2009?

5. The time is 'quarter to seven in the evening'.

   What is this time as a 24-hour clock time?

6. 31,642

   What is the number 3 worth in this number?

7. This number machine multiplies a number by 2 and subtracts 2.2.

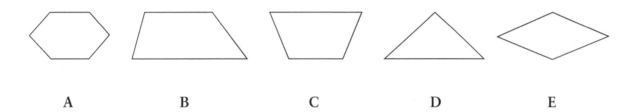

   ?   6.2

   What number must be put into the machine?

8. Which one of these shapes does **not** have any lines of symmetry?

   A   B   C   D   E

9. A magazine costs £1.35.

   How much will 6 magazines cost?

10. What are the co-ordinates of the point P?

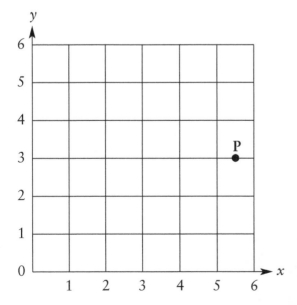

11. A bag contains 28 sweets.

Three-quarters of the sweets are toffees.

How many of the sweets are **not** toffees?

12. The average temperature was recorded for five days one week during January.

Here are the temperatures:

0°C   –3°C   –4°C   1°C   –1°C

Which is the coldest temperature?

13. Which two 3D shapes each have five faces?

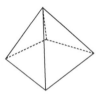   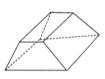

P   Q   R   S   T

14. What is the next number in the sequence?

5.2   2.6   1.3   0.65   ?

15. Which number is exactly divisible by both 9 and 12?

228   252   198   321   306

16. The jug contains orange juice.

0.2 litres of orange juice is poured into a large glass.

How many millilitres of orange juice are left in the jug?

17. There are 200 drawing pins in a box.

How many drawing pins are in 148 boxes?

18. 736.6985

What is this number when rounded to 1 decimal place?

19. Cricket balls are packed in boxes of nine.

John has 110 cricket balls.

How many boxes can he fill?

20. Which of these lengths is the shortest?

3 m   330 cm   3000 mm   300 mm   3 m 10 cm

21. Which of these is the smallest?

0.08   2.09% $\frac{1}{20}$ 2.4%   0.25

22. What is the median of this set of numbers?

6   3   5   5   6   2   2   8   9

23. Look at the number line.

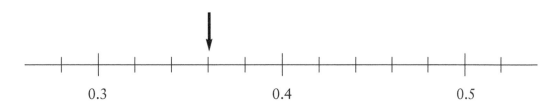

What number is the arrow pointing to?

24. Janine bought 7 pens and paid for them with a £5 note.

She was given 59p change.

What is the price of one pen?

25. Which of these angles is obtuse?

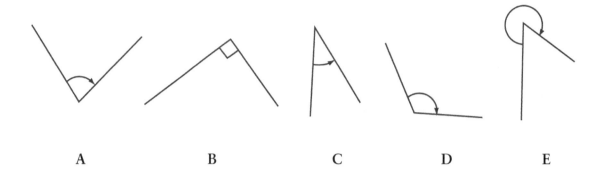

| A | B | C | D | E |

26. What is 11% of £420?

27. Which of these shapes has a different perimeter from the other four shapes?

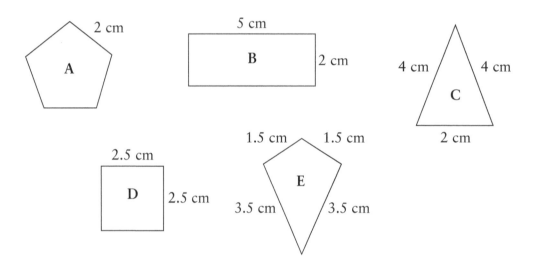

28. Here is a spinner.

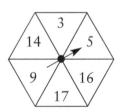

What is the probability that the spinner lands on an odd number?

29. Katy is saving to buy a new mobile phone costing £85.

She saves £6.50 a week and already has £27 in savings.

How many weeks will she have to save before she has enough money to buy the phone?

30. The graph shows the distance Patrick runs against the time it takes.

Use the graph to predict how long it will take Patrick to run 16 km.

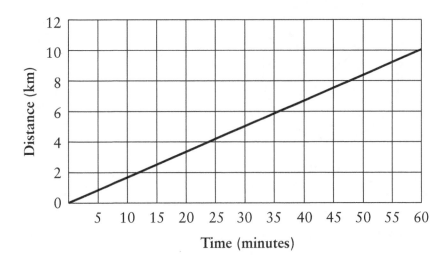

31. How many of the following shapes have two pairs of equal sides of different lengths?

kite   parallelogram   trapezium   square   rhombus

32. Here are five lines on a grid.

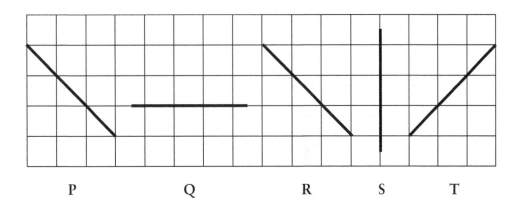

P   Q   R   S   T

Which of the following statements is **not** true?

A   P and R are parallel

B   Q is horizontal

C   P and T are parallel

D   S is vertical

E   Q is not parallel to S

33. Clock A is running 16 minutes slow. Clock B is running fast.

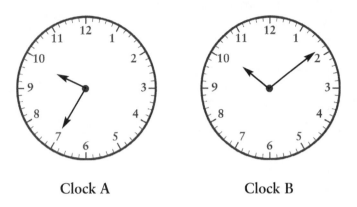

Clock A   Clock B

How many minutes fast is clock B?

34. The points P, Q and R are plotted on the grid.

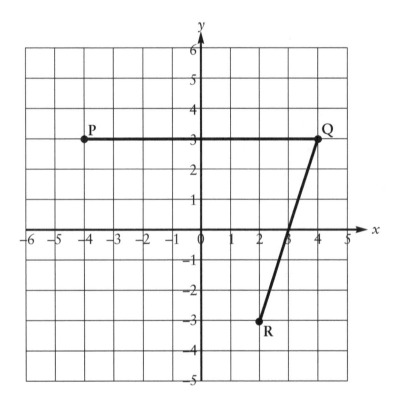

They are three of the four corners of a trapezium that has one line of symmetry.

What are the co-ordinates of point S that make the fourth corner?

35. How many small cubes have been used to make this larger cube?

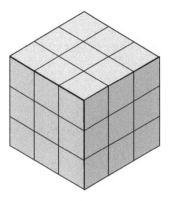

36. Andrew and Matthew share 96 sweets between them in the ratio of 5:3.

How many more sweets does Andrew get than Matthew?

37. There are 96 cars in a car park.

28 of the cars are silver.

$\frac{3}{8}$ of the cars are red.

What fraction of the cars are neither red nor silver?

38. Alice and Bryony each write down a number.

Alice's number, a, is multiplied by 5 and added to Bryony's number, b which has been multiplied by 3, to give a total of 32.

What are Alice and Bryony's numbers?

$a = 4$ and $b = 3$

$a = 5$ and $b = 2$

$a = 4$ and $b = 4$

$a = 6$ and $b = 1$

$a = 3$ and $b = 3$

39. What percentage of the shape is shaded?

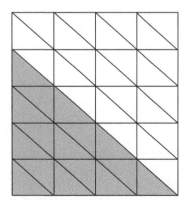

40. Imran places objects weighing 2.1 kg, 800 g and 0.45 kg on one side of a balance.

He places two objects on the other side so that both sides balance.

If one of these two objects weighs 1600 g, what is the weight of the other object in kilograms?

41. $5a + 3b - c = T$

If $a = 2$, $b = 5$ and $c = 10$, what is the value of T?

42. $5 \times 5 \times 5 \times 5 = ?$

What does ? stand for?

A 4×5

B 4^5

C 125

D 5^4

E $4 \times 4 \times 4 \times 4 \times 4$

43. Cups cost £x each and saucers cost £y each.

What is the cost of eight cups and saucers?

44. The **shaded** area in the regular pentagon is 6 cm².

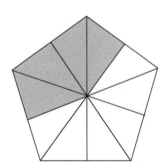

What is the total area of the regular pentagon in mm²?

15 mm²   18 mm²   150 mm²   180 mm²   1500 mm²

45. This is part of a table that can be used for converting between grams and ounces.

Grams	Ounces
24	0.85
40	1.41
5	0.18

Use the information in the table to convert 69 grams to ounces.

46. A scalene triangle has three angles, A, B and C.

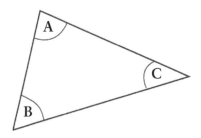

Angle A is twice the size of angle C.

Angle B is 20° smaller than A.

What is the size of angle C?

47. A large box holds 8 peaches and a small box holds 4 peaches.

Which of the following does not contain the same number of peaches as the other four?

A 2 large boxes and 4 small boxes

B 3 large boxes and 2 small boxes

C 1 large box and 6 small boxes

D 4 large boxes

E 3 large boxes and 1 small box

48. Gavin is 65 inches tall.

Which is closest to his height in metres?

1.9 m   1.5 m   1.6 m   1.3 m   1.4 m

49. $472 \times 34 = 16,048$

Which of the following is incorrect?

A $236 \times 17 = 8024$

B $16,048 \div 34 = 472$

C $236 \times 68 = 16,048$

D $471 \times 34 = 16,014$

E $34 = 16,048 \div 472$

50. The mean of five numbers is 7.

Three of the five numbers are 5, 10 and 12.

The other two numbers are the same.

What is the value of both of these numbers?

Collins

PRACTICE PAPERS

Answers and Explanations

Mathematics

Practice Test A Answers and Explanations

1. **30,474**
   3 is in the 10,000 column, 4 is in the 100 column, 7 is in the 10 column and 4 is in the units column.

2. **£5.05**
   Jake has £2 + (5 × 50p) + (3 × 10p) + (5 × 5p)
   = £2 + £2.50 + £0.30 + £0.25 = £5.05 (watch the decimal point)

3. **A**
   A quadrilateral has 4 sides. A is not a quadrilateral as it has 6 sides.

4. **£5.22**
   Cost = 9 × 58p = 522p = £5.22

5. **14**
   Modal score is the most frequent.

6. **65**
   There are 37 numbers between 46 and 84.
   Half-way is the 19th number = 65

7. **14:45**
   24-hour clock time is found by adding 12 hours to the p.m. time. 2.45 p.m. becomes 14:45

8. **48**
   A square number has two equal factors:
   $25 = 5 \times 5$; $81 = 9 \times 9$; $64 = 8 \times 8$; $16 = 4 \times 4$;
   48 does not have two equal factors

9. **£1.10**
   Carrots cost 35p × 2 = 70p; Potatoes cost 40p;
   Total cost = 70p + 40p = 110p = £1.10

10. **90**
    27 is not divisible by 5; 40, 55, 105 are not divisible by 9; 90 is divisible by 5 and 9

11. **21**
    Add a bottom row of 6 dots.

12. **1.3**
    The 3 numbers with 1 in the units column are higher than the 2 numbers with 0 in the units column. 1.3 is the highest as 3 in the $\frac{1}{10}$ column is higher than 0 and 1.

13. **D**
    D is a pyramid with a square base. A is a pyramid but with a triangular base.

14. **60**
    Number of seeds in each tray = 360 ÷ 6 = 60

15. **3.8715**
    The third decimal place must be 5 or more to round up to 3.88. The number 3.8715 = 3.87 to 2 dp.

16. **216**
    Number of small cheeseburgers = 54 ÷ 2 = 27;
    Number of large cheeseburgers = 13 + 27 = 40;
    Total = (35 + 27) + (54 + 42) + (18 + 40)
    = 62 + 96 + 58 = 216

17. **15 grams**
    Weight of the chocolates = 415 − 55 = 360 g;
    Weight of one chocolate = 360 ÷ 24 = 15 g

18. **B**
    B has exactly 2 lines of symmetry; A has 4 lines of symmetry and rotational symmetry order 4; C and D have 1 line of symmetry; E has rotational symmetry order 2 but no line symmetry.

19. **1.7**
    $1\frac{7}{10}$ has 1 in the units column and 7 in the $\frac{1}{10}$ column giving 1.7

20. **(1.6, 0.8)**
    Each division on the x-axis = 0.2 ∴ x coordinate = 1.6 (1 + 3 × 0.2); each division on the y-axis = 0.2 ∴ y coordinate = 0.8 (4 × 0.2); P is the point (1.6, 0.8). Always give x coordinate first.

21. **2.7 kg**
    1 kg = 1000 g ∴ 2700 g = 2700 ÷ 1000 = 2.7 kg

22. **16:25**
    14:55 + 1 hour = 15:55;
    15:55 + (5 mins + 25 mins) = 16:00 + 25 mins = 16:25.
    Remember that 60 mins = 1 hour

23. **936**
    Number of seeds = 52 × 18 = 936 seeds. It is quicker to work out (50 × 18) + (2 × 18) = 900 + 36 = 936 than do long multiplication.

24. **B**
    Turn the sheet to face the direction of travel in order to have correct Left and Right.

25. **B**
    60–64 = 12 people; 65–69 = 7 people; 70–74 = 5 people ⇒ total = 24 people weighing 60 kg or more

26. **60%**
    Number of girls = 30 − 12 = 18;
    % girls = 18 ÷ 30 × 100 = 60%;
    Or % boys = 12 ÷ 30 × 100 = 40%
    ∴ % girls = 100 − 40 = 60%

27. **42°C**
    Difference in temperature = 24 + 18 = 42°C

28. **280°**
    x + ? = 360°. Unknown angle is close to a right angle (90°), but isn't quite big enough.
    $x + 80° = 360°$; $360° − 80° = x$;
    $x = 280°$ approximately

29. **8**
    Total ages = 4 × 10 = 40 years;
    Age of 4th brother = 40 − (7 + 11 + 14) = 40 − 32
    = 8 years

30. **3:4**
    Number of boys = 28 − 12 = 16; girls:boys = 12:16 = 3:4. Divide by 4 to have ratio in lowest terms. Always give ratio in the order given in question.

31. **15**
    Let the number be n; $4(n + 3) − 12 = 60$; $4n + 12 − 12 = 60$; $4n = 60$; $n = 60 ÷ 4 = 15$

32. **$\frac{4}{11}$**
    Total books = 35 + 20 = 55;
    Fraction of hardbacks = $\frac{20}{55} = \frac{4}{11}$
    Divide by 5 to have fraction in lowest terms.

33. **119 cm²**
    Divide shape into two rectangles;
    Area = (9 × 6) + (5 × 13) = 54 + 65 = 119 cm²

34. **C**
    There are four 3s on spinner B and only two 3s on spinner A. Only C is true.

35. **C**
    Only K and N are equal and therefore congruent.

36. **$\frac{7}{8}$**
    The easiest method is to convert all fractions to decimals. $\frac{3}{5} = 0.6$; $\frac{3}{10} = 0.3$; $\frac{3}{4} = 0.75$; $\frac{7}{8} = 0.875$; $\frac{7}{9} = 0.777...$; 0.875 or $\frac{7}{8}$ is the highest.

37. **4.68**
    Each division = 0.02;
    Arrow points to 4.7 − 0.02 = 4.68

38. **$3t + 15$**

 Boris' age = t years; Kyle's age = $t + 5$;

 Ian's age = $3(t + 5) = 3t + 15$

39. **$\frac{1}{3}$ of 330**

 30% of 320 = 0.3 of 320 = 96; $\frac{1}{3}$ of 330 = 110; 33% of 300 = 99; $\frac{3}{10}$ of 310 = 93;

 Greatest value = $\frac{1}{3}$ of 330

40. **128 km**

 1 km ≈ $\frac{5}{8}$ mile; 80 miles ≈ $\frac{8}{5}$ × 80 = 640 ÷ 5 = 128 km

41. **£2000**

 Total money = 18 taxis × 19 fares × £5 = £1710, which gives an estimate of £2000.

42. **112**

 $16^2 - 12^2 = (16 + 12)(16 - 12) = 28 \times 4 = 112$. Or work out the squares and subtract:

 $16^2 - 12^2 = 256 - 144 = 112$

43. **C**

 Laura runs 6 × 2.35 = 14.10 km = 14 100 m;

 Ravi runs 4 × 3550 = 14 200 m;

 ∴ Ravi runs 100 m more.

44. **£200**

 Sale price = (100 – 20)% of original price = 80%(0.8) of original price; original price = £160 ÷ 0.8 = £200

45. **28 cm²**

 Perimeter of rectangle = $2(l + b) = 24 \Rightarrow l + b = 12$; area of rectangle = $l \times b$; each area given must have factors that add up to 12. Only 28 cm² does not have this.

46. **123°**

 x is the exterior angle of the triangle and equals the sum of the two opposite interior angles.

 $x = 51° + 72° = 123°$

47. **(31 × 24) + 24 = 688**

 (31 × 24) is 24 less than (32 × 24); + 24 is 104 more than – 80; (31 × 24) + 24 = 688 is incorrect. All the others can be deduced from the original.

48. **$2a + 2b + 2c$**

 Perimeter is the sum of all the sides

 $= a + b + b + a + c + c = 2a + 2b + 2c$

49. **5**

 $4n + 15 = 45 - 2n$

 $4n + 2n = 45 - 15$

 $6n = 30$

 $n = 30 \div 6 = 5$

50. **100**

 30% of the drinks = coffee = 150 cups;

 10% of the drinks = 150 ÷ 3 = 50 cups;

 % chocolate = 100 – (10 + 30 + 40) = 100 – 80 = 20%;

 chocolate = 20% of the drinks = 50 × 2 = 100 cups

Practice Test B Answers and Explanations

1. **8000**
   18,674: 8 is in the 1,000 column and is equal to 8000
2. **E**
   E is the only triangle with a right angle and is a right-angled triangle.
3. **£11.78**
   A DVD costs £19.76 – £7.98 = £11.78
4. **–12°C**
   The temperature in Moscow = –1°C – 11°C = **–12°C**
5. **75 minutes**
   The programme lasts from 15:35 to 16:50; 15:35 → 16:00 = 25 mins; 16:00 → 16:50 = 50 mins;
   Total time = 25 mins + 50 mins = 75 mins
6. **45**
   Four small squares represent 20 trees. Number of oak trees = $\frac{1}{2}$ × 20 = 10; number of birch trees = 20 + 20 + ($\frac{3}{4}$ × 20) = 20 + 20 + 15 = 55; there are 55 – 10 or 45 more birch trees than oak trees.
7. **Hexagon**
   The shape has 6 sides so is a hexagon.
8. **26,048**
   Twenty six thousand = 26,000; forty eight = 48;
   Whole number is 26,048.
9. **9**
   Factors of 24 do not include 9.
10. **105**
    525 ÷ 5 = 105
11. **B**
    Only B has 3 acute angles (angle between 0° and 90°).
12. **23**
    The sequence is generated by +5 and –2 alternately.
    The next number = 18 + 5 = 23
13. **8**
    3 children have a score of 1–5; 5 children have a score of 6–10; 8 children have a score less than 11.
14. **70**
    70 is a multiple of 2, 5, 7, 10, 14, 35, 70 not 15.
15. **E**
    Turn the sheet to face the direction of travel in order to have correct Left and Right.
16. **B**
    B as parallelograms do not have lines of symmetry.
17. **£1.30**
    He spends £3.80 + £4.90 = £8.70.
    Change = £10 – £8.70 = £1.30
18. **91**
    Thursday tickets = 52 + 63 + 21 = 136; Saturday tickets = 110 + 76 + 41 = 227; 227 – 136 = 91 more tickets are sold on Saturday.
19. **31**
    There are 13 numbers between 24 and 38.
    Half-way is the 7th number = 31.
20. **8g**
    A 50p coin weighs less than 25 g, but 1 g is too small.
    Weight is approximately 8 g
21. **£144**
    Trip will cost £26 × 18 = £468. Extra amount needed = £468 – £324 = £144
22. **(3, 1)**
    Only point (3, 1) will be on a line through C perpendicular to AB.
23. **124 m**
    Length of fencing = perimeter = 2(28 + 34)
    = 2 × 62 = 124 m
24. **C**
    A circle must be next to a shaded square. A and E are incorrect. Only C will fold to make the cube.
25. **4**
    Reverse the procedure to find the original number;
    17 – 1 = 16, 16 ÷ 4 = 4
26. **E**
    No other choice gives mint.
27. **1.36**
    Each division equals 0.02;
    arrow points to 1.4 – (2 × 0.02) = 1.4 – 0.04 = 1.36
28. **9**
    Paul's age (P) = 4 × Brother's age (B); in 6 years' time, P = 4B + 6 = 18; B = 3. In 6 years' time Paul's brother will be 3 + 6 = 9 years.
29. **14**
    Number of coaches = 448 ÷ 32 = 14
30. **4**
    Mean shoe size = total of sizes ÷ number of children
    = 36 ÷ 9 = 4
31. **100°**
    Angle a is a bit more than a right angle and is approximately 100°
32. **15%**
    The diagram has 20 triangles;
    % shaded = $\frac{3}{20}$ × 100 = 15%
33. **$\frac{9}{11}$**
    Number of white balls = 11 – (5 + 2) = 11 – 7 = 4
    P (red or white) = $\frac{5}{11} + \frac{4}{11} = \frac{9}{11}$; add probabilities as both options may occur.
34. **87 kg**
    15% of 580 kg = 0.15 × 580 = 87 kg
35. **9.22**
    9.21563 = 9.22 to 2dp as digit in 3rd dp = 5, meaning that 1 must be added to 2nd dp when correcting.
36. **475 grams**
    Each division on scale equals 50. Arrow points to half-way between 2nd and 3rd divisions, giving reading of 475 g
37. **375 grams**
    150 g makes 10 biscuits; 15 g (150 ÷ 10) makes 1 biscuit. 375 g (25 × 15) will make 25 biscuits.
38. **D**
    P: $x = –4, y = 3$; Q: $x = 2, y = –3$; D is correct
39. **D**
    $\frac{5}{6}$ = 0.8333..., $\frac{2}{3}$ = 0.666..., $\frac{3}{4}$ = 0.75, $\frac{5}{8}$ = 0.625;
    D is correct. It is easier to put in order if fractions are changed into decimals.
40. **58 cm²**
    Divide shape into 2 rectangles. Divide measurements by 10 to convert mm to cm.
    Area = (8 × 3.5) + 12(6 – 3.5) = 28 + 30 = 58 cm²
41. **2.5 km**
    1 cm represents 125,000 cm or 1.25 km;
    2 cm represent 2 × 1.25 km = 2.5 km
42. **3 hours**
    If the mean = 6 hours, total should be (6 × 6) = 36 hours. He must work 3 hours on Saturday to make the total of 36 hours.

43. **2.995**

The difference 3 – 2.995 = 0.005, which is smaller than the other differences. This means that 2.995 is the closest to 3.

44. $n - 12$

If Gemma's age = n and Claire's age = $n - 5$, then Zoe's age = $n - 5 - 7 = n - 12$

45. **243**

The numbers are powers of 3: $3^1 = 3$, $3^2 = 9$, $3^3 = 27$, $3^4 = 81$. The missing number is $3^5 = 243$

46. $\frac{3}{10}$

Divide $\frac{24}{80}$ by 8 to covert to its lowest terms.
$24 \div 8 = 3$, $80 \div 8 = 10$; $\frac{24}{80} = \frac{3}{10}$

47. **72°**

Angle sum at centre = 360°; $x = 360° \div 5 = 72°$

48. **3**

Number of days from Mar 1st to May 31st
= 31 + 30 + 31 = 92
Multiples of 9: 9, 18, 27, 36, 45, 54, 63, 72, 81, 90
Multiples of 5: 5, 10, 15, 20, 25, 30, 35, 40, 45, 50, 55, 60, 65, 70, 75, 80, 85, 90
Common multiples of 9 and 5 : 45, 90
After 1st Mar, there are two more occasions when the bins and boxes are emptied on the same day, making a total of 3.

49. $a = 5c + 2b$

$a = 5c - 2b$ not $a = 5c + 2b$

50. $xy + xz$

Area of shape = $xy + (2 \times \frac{1}{2} \times zx) = xy + xz$

Practice Test C Answers and Explanations

1. **E**
   13,045 is thirteen thousand and forty-five.
2. **8**
   Number of sunny days in June = 17; number of sunny days in August = 9; June has 8 more sunny days.
3. **D**
   D does not have 5 sides, so is not a pentagon.
4. **140**
   $560 \div 4 = 140$
5. **250 millilitres**
   A glass of milk has approximately 250 ml. 20 ml is too small and the other amounts are too large.
6. **170**
   At York, there are 8 fewer people on the train. $(67 - 59)$ making a total of 170.
7. **900**
   1 circle represents 100 CDs. On Saturday and Sunday, there are 8 full circles and 2 half circles, making 9 full circles. Total CDs = 900
8. **–9 and –16**
   The difference between the terms = –7;
   The next two terms are $-2 - 7 = -9$ and $-9 - 7 = -16$
9. **£8.20**
   He spends $2(£3.50) + £1.20 = £7 + £1.20 = £8.20$
10. **I**
    Reflections in the 2 lines make I.
11. **(3, 4.5)**
    x coordinate = 3, y coordinate = $4.5 \Rightarrow$ P is the point (3, 4.5)
12. **0.35 kg**
    Range = largest – smallest = $1.4 - 1.05 = 0.35$ kg
13. **2.98**
    The numbers all have 2 in the units column; 2.9 and 2.98 have 9 in the $\frac{1}{10}$ column, but 2.98 has 8 in the $\frac{1}{100}$ column, so is the largest number.
14. **49**
    Number = $(11 \times 6) - 17 = 49$
15. **330**
    Number of minutes = $(5 \times 60) + 30 = 330$ mins
16. **A**
    Areas: A = 4, B, C, D, E all equal 5. A is different.
17. **$\frac{15}{20}$**
    $\frac{15}{20}$ cannot be cancelled down to $\frac{4}{5}$. $\frac{15}{20} = \frac{3}{4}$ in its lowest terms.
18. **56**
    If the number is n, $(n + 12) \div 2 = 34$;
    $n + 12 = 2 \times 34 = 68$; $n = 68 - 12 = 56$
19. **B**
    After turning 180°, the vertical line should be on the LHS with the dot under the bar.
20. **20**
    10% or $\frac{1}{10}$ of 200 = 20 silver coins
21. **£3.00**
    She spends $60 \times 5p = 300p = £3$ per week
22. **14 metres**
    Actual width of room = $4 \times 3.5 = 14$ m
23. **A**
    Triangular prism: the shape is a prism with triangular cross-section.
24. **£8.95**
    Cost = $(5 \times £1.15) + (4 \times £0.80) = £5.75 + £3.20 = £8.95$
25. **112**
    Difference between the numbers = 8; $104 + 8 = 112$
26. **A**
    Each division = 45° (360° ÷ 8);
    volume 5 → volume 2 = $3 \times 45° = 135°$
27. **9 and 25**
    3rd pattern has $3 \times 3 = 9$ dots;
    5th pattern has $5 \times 5 = 25$ dots.
28. **120°**
    Exterior angle of regular hexagon = 360° ÷ 6 = 60°;
    Interior angle of regular hexagon(x) = 180° – 60° = 120°
29. **10**
    300 ml of milk has 4 spoonfuls of syrup; 150 ml of milk has 2 spoonfuls of syrup; 750 ml of milk has (2×5) or 10 spoonfuls of syrup.
30. **(2, –1)**
    QR = 6 units = PS; S is point (2, –1)
31. **£8.75**
    Sale price = $(100 - 30)$% of £12.50
    = $0.7 \times £12.50 = £8.75$
32. **$450**
    £100 = $150 ⇒ £300 = $450
33. **69**
    $\frac{3}{7} \times 161 = 69$ pepperoni pizzas
34. **$y - x = 5$**
    $y - x = 5$ gives $y = 5 + x$ not $y = 5x$
35. **$\frac{1}{6}$**
    Number of white chocolates = $24 - (12 + 8) = 4$; P (white) = $\frac{4}{24} = \frac{1}{6}$; divide by 4 to put in lowest terms.
36. **7**
    Julie needs £120 – £24 = £96; number of Saturdays worked = £96 ÷ £15.50 = 6.19. This means Julie must work 7 Saturdays to cover the cost.
37. **£7000**
    Prices in order: £5000, £5500, £6500, £7000, £7500, £7500, £8000. Median (middle) price = £7000
38. **10,800**
    Number of paperclips = $300 \times 36 = 10,800$
39. **$\frac{3}{10}$**
    Fraction = $\frac{600}{2000}$; both amounts changed to ml = $\frac{3}{10}$; divide by 200 to put in lowest terms.
40. **$7x + 8$**
    He swims $5x + 2(x + 4) = 5x + 2x + 8 = 7x + 8$ lengths.
41. **100 m²**
    Divide shape into 3 rectangles.
    Area = $2 \times (5 \times 2) + 16 \times (7 - 2) = 20 + 80 = 100$ m²
42. **15**
    Total number of ratio parts = $3 + 5 = 8$;
    1 ratio part = $24 \div 8 = 3$ children;
    number of girls = $5 \times 3 = 15$
43. **36°**
    Angle sum on a straight line = 180°;
    $5x = 180° \Rightarrow x = 180° \div 5 = 36°$
44. **8**
    $8y - 24 = 40 \Rightarrow 8y = 40 + 24 = 64$; $y = 64 \div 8 = 8$
45. **64**
    80 athletes = 25% or $\frac{1}{4}$ of total;
    Total = $4 \times 80 = 320$ athletes;
    % gold = $100 - (55 + 25) = 100 - 80 = 20$%;
    number of gold = 20% of 320 = $0.2 \times 320 = 64$
46. **$z(x + y)$**
    Area = $(z \times x) + 2 \times \frac{1}{2}(y \times z) = zx + yz = z(x + y)$

47. 13.0

When dividing by a decimal, convert to a whole number, doing the same procedure to the original number; $5.2 \div 0.4$ becomes $52 \div 4$ ($\times$ both by 10) = 13

48. 6.25 km

1 cm represents 125,000 cm or 1.25 km; 5 cm represents 5×1.25 km = 6.25 km

49. 24 cm

It is easier to mark the lengths on the shape. Perimeter = $(6 \times 20) + (3 \times 40) = 120 + 120 = 240$ mm or 24 cm

50. $2 = b + a$

$2 = b + a$ gives $a = 2 - b$ not $2a = b$

Practice Test D Answers and Explanations

1. **4590**
   4586 = 4590 to the nearest 10 as 86 is nearer to 90 than 80.

2. **230**
   Number of blue eyes = 110, number of brown eyes = 80, number of grey eyes = 40; number of non-green eyes = 110 + 80 + 40 = 230

3. **D**
   D is a pentagon with 5 sides, not a quadrilateral with 4 sides.

4. **5**
   2008 total = 22, 2009 total = 17;
   there were 5 (22 − 17) more medals in 2008.

5. **18:45**
   Quarter to seven in the evening is 6.45 p.m. Add 12 hours to the p.m. time for 24-hour time. 6.45 p.m. becomes 18:45.

6. **Thirty thousand**
   The number 3 is in the 10,000 column. Its value is 30,000.

7. **4.2**
   Reverse procedure to find original number;
   6.2 + 2.2 = 8.4 ÷ 2 = 4.2

8. **B**
   B is a trapezium with 4 different sides. It does not have lines of symmetry.

9. **£8.10**
   Cost = 6 × £1.35 = £8.10

10. **(5.5, 3)**
    x coordinate = 5.5, y coordinate = 3; P is the point (5.5,3)

11. **7**
    A quarter of the sweets are not toffees = $\frac{1}{4}$ × 28 = 7

12. **−4°C**
    The coldest temperature is −4°C. It is 4 degrees below zero.

13. **P and S**
    P and S both have 5 faces. Count carefully.

14. **0.325**
    Each term is $\frac{1}{2}$ the previous term. The next term = 0.65 ÷ 2 = 0.325.

15. **252**
    Test first term by dividing by 9. If answer is a whole number, then try 12. The next term gives 252 ÷ 9 = 28 and 252 ÷ 12 = 21. There is no need to go any further.

16. **120 ml**
    0.2 l = 200 ml; juice left = 320 − 200 = 120 ml

17. **29,600**
    Number of drawing pins = 200 × 148 = 29,600; it is easier to multiply 148 by 2 and add two noughts.

18. **736.7**
    2nd dp is 9, so add 1 to 1st dp giving 736.7

19. **12**
    110 balls will fit into 110 ÷ 9 = 12 boxes with 2 remaining balls.

20. **300 mm**
    Change all measurements to cm to compare: 300, 330, 300, 30, 310; shortest = 30 cm = 300 mm

21. **2.09%**
    Change to decimals to compare: 0.08, 0.0209, 0.05, 0.024, 0.25 or 100ths: $\frac{8}{100}$, $\frac{2.09}{100}$, $\frac{5}{100}$, $\frac{2.4}{100}$, $\frac{25}{100}$
    Smallest = 2.09%

22. **5**
    Put in order to find median (middle):
    2, 2, 3, 5, 5, 6, 6, 8, 9; median = 5

23. **0.36**
    Each division = 0.02. Arrow points to 0.36.

24. **63p**
    She spent 500 − 59 = 441; 441 ÷ 7 = 63p

25. **D**
    D is the only obtuse angle (between 90° and 180°)

26. **£46.20**
    11% of £420 = 0.11 × £420 = £46.20

27. **B**
    A, C, D, E all have a perimeter of 10 cm. B has a perimeter of 14 cm.

28. **$\frac{2}{3}$**
    There are 4 odd numbers out of 6.
    P(odd number) = $\frac{4}{6}$ = $\frac{2}{3}$; divide by 2 to have probability in lowest terms.

29. **9**
    She needs £85 − £27 = £58; number of weeks needed = £58 ÷ £6.50 = 8.9; she needs 9 weeks' savings.

30. **96 minutes**
    Patrick takes 60 mins to run 10 km. Multiply 60 by $\frac{16}{10}$ to find predicted time. He should take $\frac{16}{10}$ × 60 = 96 minutes.

31. **2**
    A square and a rhombus have 4 equal sides. A trapezium has 4 different sides. 2 shapes, a kite and a parallelogram, have 2 pairs of equal sides of different lengths.

32. **C**
    P and T are not parallel. All the other statements are true.

33. **18 minutes**
    Time on clock A should be 09:35 + 16 mins = 09:51; time on clock B is 10:09. It is 18 mins fast.

34. **(−2, −3)**
    The one line of symmetry is the y-axis giving S (−2, −3)

35. **27**
    Number of small cubes = 3 × 3 × 3 = 27

36. **24**
    Total of ratio parts = 5 + 3 = 8;
    1 ratio part = 96 ÷ 8 = 12; Andrew has 2 more parts than Matthew. He has 2 × 12 = 24 more sweets.

37. **$\frac{1}{3}$**
    Number of silver = 28; number of red = $\frac{3}{8}$ × 96 = 36; other cars = 96 − (28 +36) = 96 − 64 = 32;
    fraction of other cars = $\frac{32}{96}$ = $\frac{1}{3}$;
    divide by 32 to have fraction in lowest terms.

38. **a = 4 and b = 4**
    Substitute given values in $5a + 3b$ until total of 32 is found. a = 4, b = 4

39. **40%**
    Shaded triangles = 16; total triangles = 40;
    % shaded = $\frac{16}{40}$ × 100 = 40%

40. **1.75 kg**
    Convert all weights to kg. LHS total = 2.1 + 0.8 + 0.45 = 3.35 kg; other object weighs 3.35 − 1.6 = 1.75 kg.

41. **15**
    Substitute given values in formula: (5 × 2) + (3 × 5) − 10 = 10 + 15 − 10 = 15; T = 15

42. **D**
    5 × 5 × 5 × 5 can be written as 5^4 (4 lots of 5 multiply each other)

43. **$8x + 8y$**

Cost $= (8 \times x) + (8 \times y) = 8x + 8y$

44. **1500 mm²**

$6\,cm^2 = 600\,mm^2$; total area $= \frac{10}{4} \times 600 = 1500\,mm^2$

45. **2.44 ounces**

Left column total $= 69\,g$; right column total $= 0.85 +$
$1.41 + 0.18 = 2.44$ ounces.

46. **40°**

$A = 2C, B = A - 20°$
Angle sum of triangle $= A + B + C = 180°$
$2C + (2C - 20°) + C = 180°$
$2C + 2C + C = 180° + 20°$
$5C = 200°$
$C = 40°$

47. **E**

A: $(2 \times 8) + (4 \times 4) = 16 + 16 = 32$
B: $(3 \times 8) + (2 \times 4) = 24 + 8 = 32$
C: $(1 \times 8) + (6 \times 4) = 8 + 24 = 32$
D: $(4 \times 8) = 32$
E is different: $(3 \times 8) + (1 \times 4) = 24 + 4 = 28$

48. **1.6 m**

1 inch $\approx 2.5\,cm$: $65 \times 2.5 \approx 162.5\,cm = 1.625\,m$;
Gavin's height is approximately 1.6 m

49. **A**

If $472 \times 34 = 16{,}048$, then $236(472 \div 2) \times 17(34 \div 2)$
$= 16{,}048 \div 4 = 4012$

50. **4**

Total of the numbers $= 7 \times 5 = 35$;
other two numbers each equal $[35 - (5 + 10 + 12)] \div 2$
$= [35 - 27] \div 2 = 8 \div 2 = 4$

Notes

Notes

Notes

MATHEMATICS TEST A

Pupil's Name

School Name

Date of Test

© HarperCollinsPublishers Ltd

Please mark like this ⊢.

PUPIL NUMBER	SCHOOL NUMBER
[0] [0] [0] [0] [0] [0]	[0] [0] [0] [0] [0] [0]
[1] [1] [1] [1] [1] [1]	[1] [1] [1] [1] [1] [1]
[2] [2] [2] [2] [2] [2]	[2] [2] [2] [2] [2] [2]
[3] [3] [3] [3] [3] [3]	[3] [3] [3] [3] [3] [3]
[4] [4] [4] [4] [4] [4]	[4] [4] [4] [4] [4] [4]
[5] [5] [5] [5] [5] [5]	[5] [5] [5] [5] [5] [5]
[6] [6] [6] [6] [6] [6]	[6] [6] [6] [6] [6] [6]
[7] [7] [7] [7] [7] [7]	[7] [7] [7] [7] [7] [7]
[8] [8] [8] [8] [8] [8]	[8] [8] [8] [8] [8] [8]
[9] [9] [9] [9] [9] [9]	[9] [9] [9] [9] [9] [9]

DATE OF BIRTH

Day	Month	Year
[0] [0]	January	2007
[1] [1]	February	2008
[2] [2]	March	2009
[3] [3]	April	2010
[4]	May	2011
[5]	June	2012
[6]	July	2013
[7]	August	2014
[8]	September	2015
[9]	October	2016
	November	2017
	December	2018

1
- 34,474
- 30,704
- 30,474
- 3,474
- 30,744

2
- £5.05
- £4.05
- £4.85
- £5.00
- £2.65

3
- A
- B
- C
- D
- E

4
- £4.64
- £5.12
- £5.13
- £5.22
- £5.80

5
- 14
- 12
- 11
- 16
- 8

6
- 65
- 60
- 62
- 63
- 58

7
- 12:45
- 02:45
- 14:45
- 16:45
- 08:45

8
- 25
- 81
- 64
- 48
- 16

9
- £1.10
- £0.75
- £1.50
- £1.15
- £1.20

10
- 27
- 40
- 55
- 90
- 105

11
- 15
- 19
- 20
- 21
- 26

12
- 1.14
- 0.33
- 1.03
- 1.3
- 0.43

13
- A
- B
- C
- D
- E

14
- 36
- 60
- 6
- 42
- 48

15
- 3.8808
- 3.88402
- 3.8796
- 3.8715
- 3.875055

16
- 149
- 176
- 189
- 216
- 220

17
- 10 grams
- 12 grams
- 15 grams
- 17 grams
- 20 grams

18
- A
- B
- C
- D
- E

19
- 0.17
- 1.7
- 0.7
- 7.1
- 1.07

20
- (1.6, 0.8)
- (0.8, 1.6)
- (1.3, 0.4)
- (0.4, 1.3)
- (1.6, 0.4)

21
- 20.7 kg
- 27 kg
- 2.07 kg
- 0.27 kg
- 2.7 kg

22
- 17:25
- 16:30
- 16:25
- 15:45
- 16:15

23
- 126
- 468
- 900
- 936
- 1022

24
- A
- B
- C
- D
- E

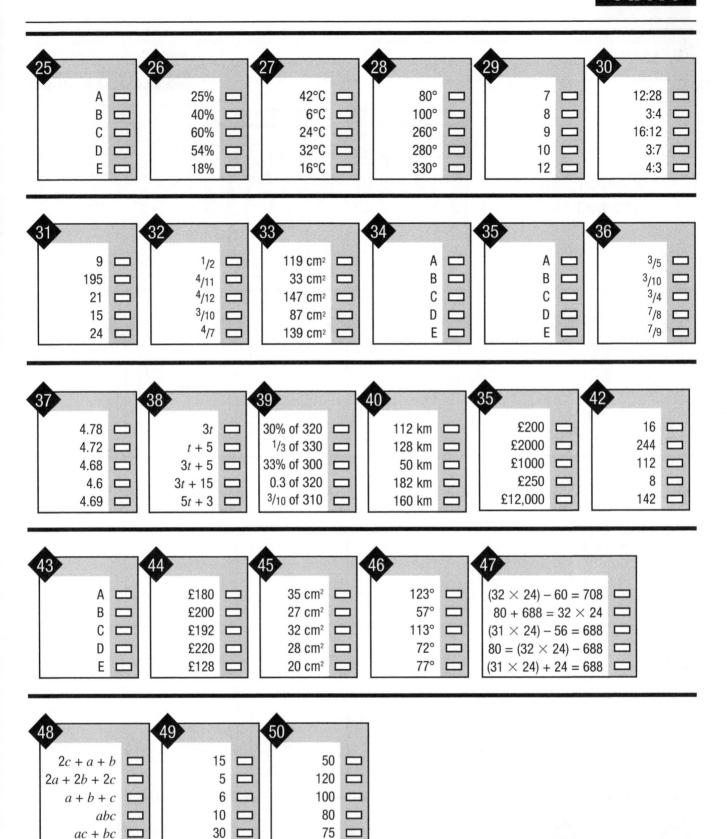

25
- A ☐
- B ☐
- C ☐
- D ☐
- E ☐

26
- 25% ☐
- 40% ☐
- 60% ☐
- 54% ☐
- 18% ☐

27
- 42°C ☐
- 6°C ☐
- 24°C ☐
- 32°C ☐
- 16°C ☐

28
- 80° ☐
- 100° ☐
- 260° ☐
- 280° ☐
- 330° ☐

29
- 7 ☐
- 8 ☐
- 9 ☐
- 10 ☐
- 12 ☐

30
- 12:28 ☐
- 3:4 ☐
- 16:12 ☐
- 3:7 ☐
- 4:3 ☐

31
- 9 ☐
- 195 ☐
- 21 ☐
- 15 ☐
- 24 ☐

32
- $1/2$ ☐
- $4/11$ ☐
- $4/12$ ☐
- $3/10$ ☐
- $4/7$ ☐

33
- 119 cm² ☐
- 33 cm² ☐
- 147 cm² ☐
- 87 cm² ☐
- 139 cm² ☐

34
- A ☐
- B ☐
- C ☐
- D ☐
- E ☐

35
- A ☐
- B ☐
- C ☐
- D ☐
- E ☐

36
- $3/5$ ☐
- $3/10$ ☐
- $3/4$ ☐
- $7/8$ ☐
- $7/9$ ☐

37
- 4.78 ☐
- 4.72 ☐
- 4.68 ☐
- 4.6 ☐
- 4.69 ☐

38
- $3t$ ☐
- $t + 5$ ☐
- $3t + 5$ ☐
- $3t + 15$ ☐
- $5t + 3$ ☐

39
- 30% of 320 ☐
- $1/3$ of 330 ☐
- 33% of 300 ☐
- 0.3 of 320 ☐
- $3/10$ of 310 ☐

40
- 112 km ☐
- 128 km ☐
- 50 km ☐
- 182 km ☐
- 160 km ☐

35
- £200 ☐
- £2000 ☐
- £1000 ☐
- £250 ☐
- £12,000 ☐

42
- 16 ☐
- 244 ☐
- 112 ☐
- 8 ☐
- 142 ☐

43
- A ☐
- B ☐
- C ☐
- D ☐
- E ☐

44
- £180 ☐
- £200 ☐
- £192 ☐
- £220 ☐
- £128 ☐

45
- 35 cm² ☐
- 27 cm² ☐
- 32 cm² ☐
- 28 cm² ☐
- 20 cm² ☐

46
- 123° ☐
- 57° ☐
- 113° ☐
- 72° ☐
- 77° ☐

47
- $(32 \times 24) - 60 = 708$ ☐
- $80 + 688 = 32 \times 24$ ☐
- $(31 \times 24) - 56 = 688$ ☐
- $80 = (32 \times 24) - 688$ ☐
- $(31 \times 24) + 24 = 688$ ☐

48
- $2c + a + b$ ☐
- $2a + 2b + 2c$ ☐
- $a + b + c$ ☐
- abc ☐
- $ac + bc$ ☐

49
- 15 ☐
- 5 ☐
- 6 ☐
- 10 ☐
- 30 ☐

50
- 50 ☐
- 120 ☐
- 100 ☐
- 80 ☐
- 75 ☐

© HarperCollins*Publishers* Ltd

MATHEMATICS TEST B

MA B

Pupil's Name

School Name

Date of Test

PUPIL NUMBER

[0]	[0]	[0]	[0]	[0]	[0]
[1]	[1]	[1]	[1]	[1]	[1]
[2]	[2]	[2]	[2]	[2]	[2]
[3]	[3]	[3]	[3]	[3]	[3]
[4]	[4]	[4]	[4]	[4]	[4]
[5]	[5]	[5]	[5]	[5]	[5]
[6]	[6]	[6]	[6]	[6]	[6]
[7]	[7]	[7]	[7]	[7]	[7]
[8]	[8]	[8]	[8]	[8]	[8]
[9]	[9]	[9]	[9]	[9]	[9]

SCHOOL NUMBER

[0]	[0]	[0]	[0]	[0]	[0]
[1]	[1]	[1]	[1]	[1]	[1]
[2]	[2]	[2]	[2]	[2]	[2]
[3]	[3]	[3]	[3]	[3]	[3]
[4]	[4]	[4]	[4]	[4]	[4]
[5]	[5]	[5]	[5]	[5]	[5]
[6]	[6]	[6]	[6]	[6]	[6]
[7]	[7]	[7]	[7]	[7]	[7]
[8]	[8]	[8]	[8]	[8]	[8]
[9]	[9]	[9]	[9]	[9]	[9]

DATE OF BIRTH

Day		Month		Year	
	[0]	[0]	January	2007	
	[1]	[1]	February	2008	
	[2]	[2]	March	2009	
	[3]	[3]	April	2010	
		[4]	May	2011	
		[5]	June	2012	
		[6]	July	2013	
		[7]	August	2014	
		[8]	September	2015	
		[9]	October	2016	
			November	2017	
			December	2018	

Please mark like this ⊟.

1
- 800
- 80,000
- 8000
- 80
- 8

2
- A
- B
- C
- D
- E

3
- £11.78
- £12.02
- £11.74
- £11.76
- £12.24

4
- −10°C
- 10°C
- −12°C
- −13°C
- 12°C

5
- 15 minutes
- 85 minutes
- 75 minutes
- 45 minutes
- 25 minutes

6
- 65
- 45
- 9
- 55
- 10

7
- quadrilateral
- trapezium
- hexagon
- pentagon
- prism

8
- 20,648
- 26,048
- 26,480
- 26,408
- 2,648

9
- 5
- 6
- 7
- 9
- 10

10
- 100
- 101
- 105
- 11
- 10

11
- A
- B
- C
- D
- E

12
- 23
- 16
- 25
- 21
- 20

13
- 8
- 5
- 3
- 10
- 12

14
- 30
- 90
- 70
- 75
- 45

15
- A
- B
- C
- D
- E

16
- A
- B
- C
- D
- E

17
- £6.20
- £1.85
- £1.30
- £0.65
- £1.10

18
- 68
- 91
- 127
- 136
- 227

19
- 31
- 30
- 29
- 32
- 25

20
- 200 grams
- 8 grams
- 1 gram
- 40 grams
- 800 grams

21
- £196
- £298
- £468
- £144
- £36

22
- (3, 1)
- (5, 7)
- (6, 1)
- (1, 3)
- (4, 3)

23
- 124 m
- 952 m
- 62 m
- 90 m
- 96 m

24
- A
- B
- C
- D
- E

© HarperCollins Publishers Ltd

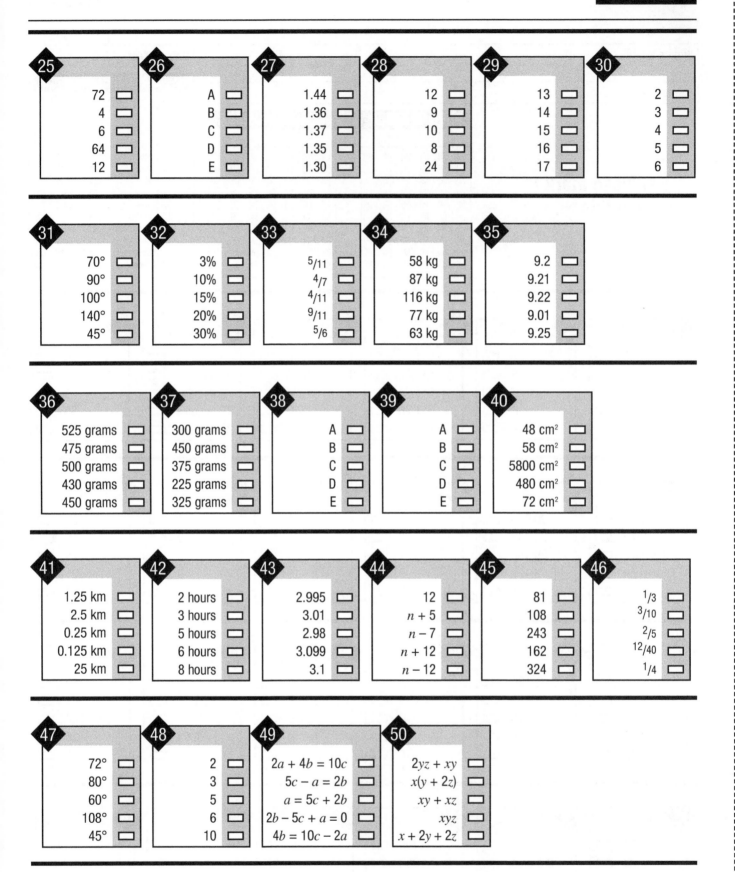

25 72 ☐ | 4 ☐ | 6 ☐ | 64 ☐ | 12 ☐

26 A ☐ | B ☐ | C ☐ | D ☐ | E ☐

27 1.44 ☐ | 1.36 ☐ | 1.37 ☐ | 1.35 ☐ | 1.30 ☐

28 12 ☐ | 9 ☐ | 10 ☐ | 8 ☐ | 24 ☐

29 13 ☐ | 14 ☐ | 15 ☐ | 16 ☐ | 17 ☐

30 2 ☐ | 3 ☐ | 4 ☐ | 5 ☐ | 6 ☐

31 70° ☐ | 90° ☐ | 100° ☐ | 140° ☐ | 45° ☐

32 3% ☐ | 10% ☐ | 15% ☐ | 20% ☐ | 30% ☐

33 $5/11$ ☐ | $4/7$ ☐ | $4/11$ ☐ | $9/11$ ☐ | $5/6$ ☐

34 58 kg ☐ | 87 kg ☐ | 116 kg ☐ | 77 kg ☐ | 63 kg ☐

35 9.2 ☐ | 9.21 ☐ | 9.22 ☐ | 9.01 ☐ | 9.25 ☐

36 525 grams ☐ | 475 grams ☐ | 500 grams ☐ | 430 grams ☐ | 450 grams ☐

37 300 grams ☐ | 450 grams ☐ | 375 grams ☐ | 225 grams ☐ | 325 grams ☐

38 A ☐ | B ☐ | C ☐ | D ☐ | E ☐

39 A ☐ | B ☐ | C ☐ | D ☐ | E ☐

40 48 cm² ☐ | 58 cm² ☐ | 5800 cm² ☐ | 480 cm² ☐ | 72 cm² ☐

41 1.25 km ☐ | 2.5 km ☐ | 0.25 km ☐ | 0.125 km ☐ | 25 km ☐

42 2 hours ☐ | 3 hours ☐ | 5 hours ☐ | 6 hours ☐ | 8 hours ☐

43 2.995 ☐ | 3.01 ☐ | 2.98 ☐ | 3.099 ☐ | 3.1 ☐

44 12 ☐ | $n+5$ ☐ | $n-7$ ☐ | $n+12$ ☐ | $n-12$ ☐

45 81 ☐ | 108 ☐ | 243 ☐ | 162 ☐ | 324 ☐

46 $1/3$ ☐ | $3/10$ ☐ | $2/5$ ☐ | $12/40$ ☐ | $1/4$ ☐

47 72° ☐ | 80° ☐ | 60° ☐ | 108° ☐ | 45° ☐

48 2 ☐ | 3 ☐ | 5 ☐ | 6 ☐ | 10 ☐

49 $2a+4b=10c$ ☐ | $5c-a=2b$ ☐ | $a=5c+2b$ ☐ | $2b-5c+a=0$ ☐ | $4b=10c-2a$ ☐

50 $2yz+xy$ ☐ | $x(y+2z)$ ☐ | $xy+xz$ ☐ | xyz ☐ | $x+2y+2z$ ☐

© HarperCollinsPublishers Ltd

MATHEMATICS TEST C

Pupil's Name

School Name

Date of Test

© HarperCollins*Publishers* Ltd

PUPIL NUMBER

[0]	[0]	[0]	[0]	[0]	[0]
[1]	[1]	[1]	[1]	[1]	[1]
[2]	[2]	[2]	[2]	[2]	[2]
[3]	[3]	[3]	[3]	[3]	[3]
[4]	[4]	[4]	[4]	[4]	[4]
[5]	[5]	[5]	[5]	[5]	[5]
[6]	[6]	[6]	[6]	[6]	[6]
[7]	[7]	[7]	[7]	[7]	[7]
[8]	[8]	[8]	[8]	[8]	[8]
[9]	[9]	[9]	[9]	[9]	[9]

SCHOOL NUMBER

[0]	[0]	[0]	[0]	[0]	[0]	[0]
[1]	[1]	[1]	[1]	[1]	[1]	[1]
[2]	[2]	[2]	[2]	[2]	[2]	[2]
[3]	[3]	[3]	[3]	[3]	[3]	[3]
[4]	[4]	[4]	[4]	[4]	[4]	[4]
[5]	[5]	[5]	[5]	[5]	[5]	[5]
[6]	[6]	[6]	[6]	[6]	[6]	[6]
[7]	[7]	[7]	[7]	[7]	[7]	[7]
[8]	[8]	[8]	[8]	[8]	[8]	[8]
[9]	[9]	[9]	[9]	[9]	[9]	[9]

DATE OF BIRTH

Day		Month		Year	
[0]	[0]	January		2007	
[1]	[1]	February		2008	
[2]	[2]	March		2009	
[3]	[3]	April		2010	
	[4]	May		2011	
	[5]	June		2012	
	[6]	July		2013	
	[7]	August		2014	
	[8]	September		2015	
	[9]	October		2016	
		November		2017	
		December		2018	

Please mark like this ⊢.

1
- A
- B
- C
- D
- E

2
- 9
- 17
- 7
- 10
- 8

3
- A
- B
- C
- D
- E

4
- 140
- 130
- 132
- 14
- 160

5
- 2 litres
- 250 millilitres
- 5 litres
- 800 millilitres
- 20 millilitres

6
- 304
- 245
- 237
- 170
- 186

7
- 1400
- 550
- 350
- 800
- 900

8
- −9 and −17
- −9 and −16
- −10 and −17
- −5 and −12
- 5 and 12

9
- £8.20
- £5.90
- £9.40
- £4.70
- £8.50

10
- E
- I
- L
- T
- F

11
- (3, 4)
- (4, 3)
- (3.5, 4)
- (3, 4.5)
- (3, 5)

12
- 0.35 kg
- 0.3 kg
- 0.2 kg
- 1.35 kg
- 0.15 kg

13
- 2.89
- 2.9
- 2.98
- 2.08
- 2.0

14
- 83
- 51
- 49
- 77
- 53

15
- 330
- 300
- 325
- 360
- 345

16
- A
- B
- C
- D
- E

17
- $8/10$
- $15/20$
- $16/20$
- $40/50$
- $20/25$

18
- 56
- 68
- 46
- 29
- 80

19
- A
- B
- C
- D
- E

20
- 180
- 20
- 10
- 2
- 40

21
- £30.00
- £2.00
- £5.00
- £3.00
- £2.50

22
- 11.5 metres
- 12 metres
- 14 metres
- 13 metres
- 7 metres

23
- A
- B
- C
- D
- E

24
- £8.95
- £9.00
- £5.25
- £8.60
- £4.35

25
116	☐
108	☐
110	☐
88	☐
112	☐

26
A	☐
B	☐
C	☐
D	☐
E	☐

27
6 and 20	☐
8 and 25	☐
9 and 25	☐
9 and 36	☐
16 and 25	☐

28
45°	☐
160°	☐
100°	☐
60°	☐
120°	☐

29
5	☐
8	☐
10	☐
12	☐
15	☐

30
$(3, -1)$	☐
$(-1, 2)$	☐
$(2, -1)$	☐
$(3, -2)$	☐
$(6, -1)$	☐

31
£11.25	☐
£9.50	☐
£3.75	☐
£8.75	☐
£10.00	☐

32
$150	☐
$300	☐
$65	☐
$200	☐
$450	☐

33
65	☐
69	☐
23	☐
43	☐
53	☐

34
$x = \frac{y}{5}$	☐
$\frac{y}{x} = 5$	☐
$10x = 2y$	☐
$y - x = 5$	☐
$0.2y = x$	☐

35
$1/3$	☐
$1/6$	☐
$1/12$	☐
$4/20$	☐
$1/2$	☐

36
7	☐
9	☐
8	☐
6	☐
5	☐

37
£5500	☐
£7500	☐
£7000	☐
£3000	☐
£6500	☐

38
10,800	☐
1800	☐
9200	☐
1080	☐
12,000	☐

39
$3/10$	☐
$1/3$	☐
$3/5$	☐
$5/6$	☐
$1/4$	☐

40
$7x$	☐
$5x + 4$	☐
$7x + 8$	☐
$7x + 4$	☐
$5x$	☐

41
35 m²	☐
100 m²	☐
90 m²	☐
112 m²	☐
105 m²	☐

42
9	☐
10	☐
8	☐
15	☐
12	☐

43
36°	☐
45°	☐
30°	☐
50°	☐
32°	☐

44
5	☐
2	☐
8	☐
7	☐
6	☐

45
16	☐
32	☐
64	☐
80	☐
88	☐

46
$x + y + z$	☐
$z(x + y)$	☐
$x(y + z)$	☐
$xz + 2yz$	☐
xyz	☐

47
2.08	☐
1.3	☐
6.5	☐
0.2	☐
13.0	☐

48
6.25 km	☐
62.5 km	☐
112.5 km	☐
6.5 km	☐
5.25 km	☐

49
24 cm	☐
240 cm	☐
260 mm	☐
220 mm	☐
20 cm	☐

50
$a + a = b$	☐
$4a = 2b$	☐
$2 = b + a$	☐
$a = 0.5b$	☐
$b = 2a$	☐

© HarperCollins*Publishers* Ltd

Pupil's Name

School Name

Date of Test

Please mark like this ⊢.

PUPIL NUMBER

[0]	[0]	[0]	[0]	[0]	[0]
[1]	[1]	[1]	[1]	[1]	[1]
[2]	[2]	[2]	[2]	[2]	[2]
[3]	[3]	[3]	[3]	[3]	[3]
[4]	[4]	[4]	[4]	[4]	[4]
[5]	[5]	[5]	[5]	[5]	[5]
[6]	[6]	[6]	[6]	[6]	[6]
[7]	[7]	[7]	[7]	[7]	[7]
[8]	[8]	[8]	[8]	[8]	[8]
[9]	[9]	[9]	[9]	[9]	[9]

SCHOOL NUMBER

[0]	[0]	[0]	[0]	[0]	[0]	[0]
[1]	[1]	[1]	[1]	[1]	[1]	[1]
[2]	[2]	[2]	[2]	[2]	[2]	[2]
[3]	[3]	[3]	[3]	[3]	[3]	[3]
[4]	[4]	[4]	[4]	[4]	[4]	[4]
[5]	[5]	[5]	[5]	[5]	[5]	[5]
[6]	[6]	[6]	[6]	[6]	[6]	[6]
[7]	[7]	[7]	[7]	[7]	[7]	[7]
[8]	[8]	[8]	[8]	[8]	[8]	[8]
[9]	[9]	[9]	[9]	[9]	[9]	[9]

DATE OF BIRTH

Day		Month		Year	
[0]	[0]	January	▭	2007	▭
[1]	[1]	February	▭	2008	▭
[2]	[2]	March	▭	2009	▭
[3]	[3]	April	▭	2010	▭
	[4]	May	▭	2011	▭
	[5]	June	▭	2012	▭
	[6]	July	▭	2013	▭
	[7]	August	▭	2014	▭
	[8]	September	▭	2015	▭
	[9]	October	▭	2016	▭
		November	▭	2017	▭
		December	▭	2018	▭

1
- 4590 ▭
- 4600 ▭
- 4580 ▭
- 4500 ▭
- 4509 ▭

2
- 30 ▭
- 60 ▭
- 230 ▭
- 220 ▭
- 260 ▭

3
- A ▭
- B ▭
- C ▭
- D ▭
- E ▭

4
- 5 ▭
- 4 ▭
- 11 ▭
- 3 ▭
- 8 ▭

5
- 07:45 ▭
- 18:45 ▭
- 06:45 ▭
- 17:45 ▭
- 18:15 ▭

6
- Thirty thousand ▭
- Thirty ▭
- Three ▭
- Three hundred ▭
- Three thousand ▭

7
- 42 ▭
- 8 ▭
- 4.2 ▭
- 2 ▭
- 8.4 ▭

8
- A ▭
- B ▭
- C ▭
- D ▭
- E ▭

9
- £6.75 ▭
- £5.40 ▭
- £6.85 ▭
- £8.20 ▭
- £8.10 ▭

10
- (6, 3) ▭
- (5.5, 4) ▭
- (5.5, 3) ▭
- (3, 6) ▭
- (5.5, 3.5) ▭

11
- 10 ▭
- 9 ▭
- 21 ▭
- 7 ▭
- 14 ▭

12
- 0°C ▭
- −3°C ▭
- −4°C ▭
- 1°C ▭
- −1°C ▭

13
- R and T ▭
- P and S ▭
- P and Q ▭
- S and T ▭
- Q and S ▭

14
- 0.35 ▭
- 0.325 ▭
- 0.32 ▭
- 0.3 ▭
- 0.333 ▭

15
- 228 ▭
- 252 ▭
- 198 ▭
- 321 ▭
- 306 ▭

16
- 120 ml ▭
- 110 ml ▭
- 300 ml ▭
- 125 ml ▭
- 200 ml ▭

17
- 14,800 ▭
- 28,600 ▭
- 14,600 ▭
- 32,000 ▭
- 29,600 ▭

18
- 737.0 ▭
- 7 ▭
- 736.7 ▭
- 736.6 ▭
- 7.3 ▭

19
- 9 ▭
- 10 ▭
- 12 ▭
- 13 ▭
- 14 ▭

20
- 3 m ▭
- 330 cm ▭
- 3000 mm ▭
- 300 mm ▭
- 3 m 10 cm ▭

21
- 0.08 ▭
- 2.09% ▭
- $1/20$ ▭
- 2.4% ▭
- 0.25 ▭

22
- 4 ▭
- 5 ▭
- 6 ▭
- 7 ▭
- 9 ▭

© HarperCollinsPublishers Ltd

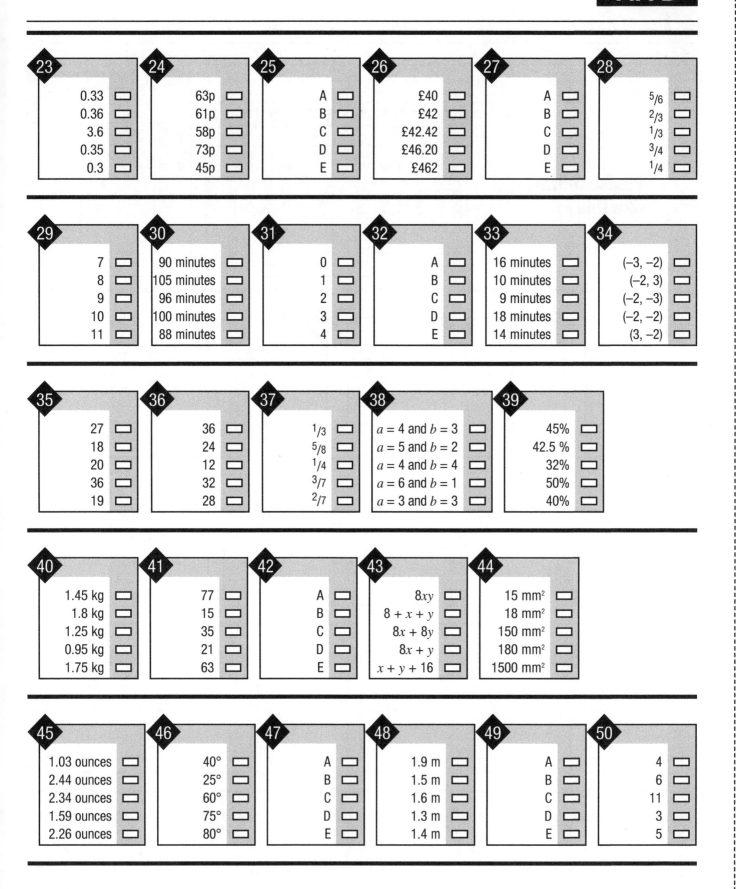

23
- 0.33 ☐
- 0.36 ☐
- 3.6 ☐
- 0.35 ☐
- 0.3 ☐

24
- 63p ☐
- 61p ☐
- 58p ☐
- 73p ☐
- 45p ☐

25
- A ☐
- B ☐
- C ☐
- D ☐
- E ☐

26
- £40 ☐
- £42 ☐
- £42.42 ☐
- £46.20 ☐
- £462 ☐

27
- A ☐
- B ☐
- C ☐
- D ☐
- E ☐

28
- $5/6$ ☐
- $2/3$ ☐
- $1/3$ ☐
- $3/4$ ☐
- $1/4$ ☐

29
- 7 ☐
- 8 ☐
- 9 ☐
- 10 ☐
- 11 ☐

30
- 90 minutes ☐
- 105 minutes ☐
- 96 minutes ☐
- 100 minutes ☐
- 88 minutes ☐

31
- 0 ☐
- 1 ☐
- 2 ☐
- 3 ☐
- 4 ☐

32
- A ☐
- B ☐
- C ☐
- D ☐
- E ☐

33
- 16 minutes ☐
- 10 minutes ☐
- 9 minutes ☐
- 18 minutes ☐
- 14 minutes ☐

34
- (−3, −2) ☐
- (−2, 3) ☐
- (−2, −3) ☐
- (−2, −2) ☐
- (3, −2) ☐

35
- 27 ☐
- 18 ☐
- 20 ☐
- 36 ☐
- 19 ☐

36
- 36 ☐
- 24 ☐
- 12 ☐
- 32 ☐
- 28 ☐

37
- $1/3$ ☐
- $5/8$ ☐
- $1/4$ ☐
- $3/7$ ☐
- $2/7$ ☐

38
- $a = 4$ and $b = 3$ ☐
- $a = 5$ and $b = 2$ ☐
- $a = 4$ and $b = 4$ ☐
- $a = 6$ and $b = 1$ ☐
- $a = 3$ and $b = 3$ ☐

39
- 45% ☐
- 42.5 % ☐
- 32% ☐
- 50% ☐
- 40% ☐

40
- 1.45 kg ☐
- 1.8 kg ☐
- 1.25 kg ☐
- 0.95 kg ☐
- 1.75 kg ☐

41
- 77 ☐
- 15 ☐
- 35 ☐
- 21 ☐
- 63 ☐

42
- A ☐
- B ☐
- C ☐
- D ☐
- E ☐

43
- $8xy$ ☐
- $8 + x + y$ ☐
- $8x + 8y$ ☐
- $8x + y$ ☐
- $x + y + 16$ ☐

44
- 15 mm² ☐
- 18 mm² ☐
- 150 mm² ☐
- 180 mm² ☐
- 1500 mm² ☐

45
- 1.03 ounces ☐
- 2.44 ounces ☐
- 2.34 ounces ☐
- 1.59 ounces ☐
- 2.26 ounces ☐

46
- 40° ☐
- 25° ☐
- 60° ☐
- 75° ☐
- 80° ☐

47
- A ☐
- B ☐
- C ☐
- D ☐
- E ☐

48
- 1.9 m ☐
- 1.5 m ☐
- 1.6 m ☐
- 1.3 m ☐
- 1.4 m ☐

49
- A ☐
- B ☐
- C ☐
- D ☐
- E ☐

50
- 4 ☐
- 6 ☐
- 11 ☐
- 3 ☐
- 5 ☐

© HarperCollins*Publishers* Ltd